POETRY EMOTIONS

Eastern England
Edited by Sarah Washer

First published in Great Britain in 2016 by:

Young Writers

Remus House
Coltsfoot Drive
Peterborough
PE2 9BF
Telephone: 01733 890066
Website: www.youngwriters.co.uk
All Rights Reserved
Book Design by Ashley Janson
© Copyright Contributors 2016
SB ISBN 978-1-78624-227-3

Printed and bound in the UK by BookPrintingUK
Website: www.bookprintinguk.com

Foreword

Welcome, Reader!

For Young Writers' latest competition, *Poetry Emotions*, we gave school children nationwide the task of writing a poem all about emotions, and they rose to the challenge magnificently!

Pupils could either write about emotions they've felt themselves or create a character to represent an emotion. Which one they chose was entirely up them. Our aspiring poets have also developed their creative skills along the way, getting to grips with poetic techniques such as rhyme, simile and alliteration to bring their thoughts to life. The result is this entertaining collection that allows us a fascinating glimpse into the minds of the next generation, giving us an insight into their innermost feelings. It also makes a great keepsake for years to come.

Here at Young Writers our aim is to encourage creativity in children and to inspire a love of the written word, so it's great to get such an amazing response, with some absolutely fantastic poems. This made it a tough challenge to pick the winners, so well done to *Honey Rotchell* who has been chosen as the best author in this anthology.

I'd like to congratulate all the young authors in *Poetry Emotions – Eastern England* – I hope this inspires them to continue with their creative writing.

Jenni Bannister

Editorial Manager

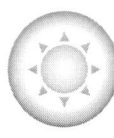

Our charity partner for this academic year is ...

YOUNGMINDS

The voice for young people's mental health and wellbeing

We're aiming to raise a huge £5,000 this academic year to help raise awareness for YoungMinds and the great work they do to support children and young people.

If you would like to get involved visit
www.justgiving.com/Young-Writers

YoungMinds is the UK's leading charity committed to improving the emotional wellbeing and mental health of children and young people. They campaign, research and influence policy and practice on behalf of children and young people to improve care and services. They also provide expert knowledge to professionals, parents and young people through the Parents' Helpline, online resources, training and development, outreach work and publications. Their mission is to improve the emotional resilience of all children and to ensure that those who suffer ill mental health get fast and effective support.

www.youngminds.org.uk

Contents

Archbishop Cranmer Academy, Nottingham

Alex Turnbull (10)	1
Alexander Munn	2
Sophie Rowe (8)	3
Lucy Taylor (9)	4
Molly Ashton (9)	4
Mya Rose Edwards (10)	5
Zac Hardy (8)	5
Florence Olivia Sudborough (9)	6
Florrie Ryan	6
Frances Dodders	7
Connie Storer (10)	7
Charlie North	8
Demi-Leigh Simpson	8
Charlie Rains	9
Jessica Scott	9
Arthur Dexter	10
Serena Lee	10
Sonny Towle	11
Evie May Adu (9)	11
Emily Wade	12
Ethan Hose	12
Libby Kennedy	13
Jenson Daubrah-Scott	13
Matthew Wyatt	14
Matthew Ward	14
Joseph Hare-Goss	15

Boston St Mary's RC Primary School, Boston

Filip Majchrzak (11)	15
Charlotte Fowlston	16
Aine Larkin (10)	16
Carrianne Elisabeth Woods (10)	17
Maria Do Mar Albuquerque	17
Saida Sakalauskaite	18
Andreia Bark	18
Ian Apilado	19
Taniya Jiyo	19
Gabriel Vallido	20
Hannah Sugg	20
Esme Brown	21
Khim Stokes	21
Danielle Gray	22
Frazer Steadman (10)	22
Ethan Anthony Blakey (11)	23
Justin Jheo Cafe-Ebuen	23
Abel Reji (9)	24
Joash Thomas (8)	24
Ziyad Rehan	25
Sophie Hannah Brown (10)	25
Rico Bringeman	26
Mollie Jeanne Fitzgerald (10)	26
Grace Bartram	27
Godwin Kozhukkullikkaran-Biji (8)	27
Angelika Kaczar	28
Oliwia Banasiuk	28
Oscar Gleeson-Garrard	29
Anielis Kvedaravicius	29
Patryk Godzisz	30
Brian Fernandes (11)	30
Mikayla Parangalan	31
Daniela Bringeman	32
Alex Barsby (8)	32
Patrick McNally (8)	33
Louise Lerin Luck (9)	33
Leon Przybylo	34
Patryk Cieslak (8)	34
Jane Margaret Caldwell	35
Godson Kozhukkullikkaran-Biji	35
Connor Blakey	36
Sophia Brigden	36
Stefano Fiore	37
Filip Dlugolecki	37
Zuzanna Bogusz	38
Joshua Mathews	38
Lilly Ireland	39
Megan O'Connor	39
Finnley Danby (9)	40
Sasha/Aleksandrs Materevs (8)	40
Dawid Machnik	41
Igor Polakov	41

Christ The King RC Primary School, Leicester

Matilda Lockton (8)	42
Zach Woolley (8)	42
Darryl Reyes (8)	43
Verity Havenhand (8)	43
Maya Joseph-Casas (8)	44
Evie Wenlock	44
Amber Bartholomew	45
Braydon Andrea Contina (8)	45
Jaime John (8)	46
Sharndre Garrity (9)	46
Felix Kennedy (8)	47
Luke Gibson (9)	47
Hannah Grace Michaluk (9)	48
Steven Darko	48
Benedict Mathew	49
Tara Lacar	49
Hannah Philip	50
Karolina Mocko	50
Lana Wood (9)	51
Alice Wakely (8)	51
Isaac Harry Warren (9)	52
Leona Boby (8)	52
Joshua Botterill (8)	53

Coltishall Primary School, Norwich

Hetty Life	53
Kenneth Frost	54
Noah Christian Smith	54
Grace Baynes (10)	55
George Parkerson	55
Honey Beatrice Rotchell (10)	56
Max Westmorland	56
Oz Kemp	57
Lucy Papworth	57
James Marshall (10)	58
Sophia Stevens	58
Ayten Kazemaliloo	59
Ellie Loiez	59
Charlie Jones	60
Leo Pearce	60
Annabel Jameson	61
Harrison Brooks	61
Toby Spalding (9)	62
Daisy Lewin	62

Fig Tree Primary School, Nottingham

Maryam Sageer (9)	63
Mustafa Siraj Uddin Hussain (8)	64
Haaris Minhas (8)	65
Maria Zainab (7)	66
Izaan Khan	67
Mohammad Isa Shahid (8)	68
Zaynab Binte Haider (8)	68
Noor-Ul-Ain Ahmed (8)	69
Ruqqaya Karam-Noor Shiekh (8)	69
Daniyal Imran (7)	70
Muneer Raza (8)	70

Harby CE Primary School, Melton Mowbray

Rose Hardiman	71
Aisling Eliza Giltinan (10)	72
Millie May Jessica Coles	73
Thomas Bosley	74
Lola Sealey (10)	74

Hasland Junior School, Chesterfield

Olivia Sian Martin (10)	75
Hannah Jeanie Smithson (11)	75

Hethersett VC Junior School, Norwich

Alex Smith (11)	76
Millie Bambridge	77
Ben Johnson (10)	78
Ellen Whiting	79
Abigail Astriani O'Dell (11)	80
Bea Boyce	81
James Attfield	82
Ruby Raynor	83
Katie Banfield	84
Lilly Walker	85
Rebecca Smith	86
Lucas Scott	87
Evie Sayer (11)	88
Lily Cook	89
Gracie Brand	90
Charlie Kate Skinner (9)	91
Isabel Younger	92
Maisie Wells (8)	92
Liam Stevens	93

Vaughan Walker (9)	93
Oliver Battley	94
Zoe Rodgers (8)	94
Evie Wood	95
Jacob Want (10)	95
Keira Hanrahan	96
Luke Howland	96
Pedro Daniel Weresi (9)	97
Henry Jack Bailie (10)	97
Cobie Mark Didwell (10)	98
Simone Awbery	98
Alex Amos	99
Ryan Walford	99
Alfie Baker	100
Toby Dunne (8)	100
Leo Jones	101
Olivia Partner (9)	101
Toby O'Dell (9)	102
Luca Foster	102
Harry Lacey (9)	103
Eleanor Ashling	103
Elizabeth Barton	104
Marcia Holbrook	104
Ellis James Bane (10)	105
Kai Codie Clayton Gray-Williams (10)	105
Demi Wright	106
Tallulah May Blake (9)	106
Jamie Alexandra Reid (9)	107
Keira Stephens (8)	107
Kyle Reeve	108
Miya Porter (9)	108
Lilia Violet Mercer (10)	109
Riley Copeland (8)	109
Mia Evie Poll (10)	110
Leo Mallett (9)	110
Isabella Williams	111
Isabella Grace Brown (8)	111
Harry Garland Goddard (10)	112
George Simmonds (8)	112
Holly Rose Palin (10)	113
Brogan Hood (8)	113
Grace Hawkins	114
Maryam Gillis (8)	114
Dayna Kelly Arbon (9)	115
Elizabeth Ottaway	115
Hannah Cox	116
Alex Scott (8)	116
Thomas Small	117
Amelia Graver	117
Maisie Beckett (11)	118
Chloe Hayes (8)	118
Ryan Turner	119
Daniel Wengrow (8)	119
Jay Vanhinsbergh (9)	120
Toby Want (10)	120
Harrison James Corr (9)	121
Kieran Poundall	121
Amy Gorman	122
Thomas Agnew	122
Abigail Conway	123
Chloe Youngs (9)	123
Kassidy Howell	124
Tom Barnard	124
Sam Cozens	125
Matthew Jacob Basham (10)	125
Milly Lightwing	126
Melissa Battley (8)	126
Dylan Nair (9)	127
Gracie Lilian Chalcraft (10)	127
Harriet Lewis	128
Nia Peres	128
Lewis Duale (10)	129
Sara Barulho Rebocho Verweij (8)	129
Toby Cawdron (9)	130
Grace Cole (9)	130
Rebecca Birchall (10)	131
Elizabeth Sharpe	131
Jasmine Swenson (9)	132
Hannah Ayu O'Dell (8)	132
Joseph Mares	133
Layla Mai Watts (8)	133
Tom Tooley	134
Harry Cheal (8)	134
Adam Abu-Elmagd (10)	135
Oliver Watson	135
Keela Ailis Olive	136
Jack Barnard	136
Lucy Ann Bradford (9)	137
Madeleine Houlihan (9)	137
Maria Kenny	138
Joshua Wright	138
Oskar Krolak	139
Ioan Warren	139
Gemma Walford	140

Isaac Lawson Ford (9)	141
Johnny Henri (8)	141
Lucy Tull (8)	142
Gabriel Escalera	142
Erin Barrett (8)	143

Radford Primary School, Nottingham

Nyesha Moran	143
Zain Afzal (9)	144
Ellie Butler	144
Tayezja Engelmann	145
Jamarne Ramone Richards (10)	145
Zain Ali	146
Trey Luke Barrett-Griffiths	146
Ayaan Khan	147
Humayd Muhammad	147
Sara Benarab	148
Aaqib Basit Muhammad (10)	148
Joshua Dzima	149
Emilia Diduch	149
Shemaraye Colbourne-Smith (10)	150
Ami Zogaj (10)	150
Kasra Khalilipir	151
Taryn Blackband	151

St Michael's VA Junior School, Norwich

Tyler Gordon (11)	152
Candece Kerslake (11)	153
Natalia Witucka (11)	154
Teagan Berry (11)	155
Alexis Venzon (11)	155
Isla Sistern (11)	156
Lillia Bettcher (11)	156

St Sebastian's CE Primary School, Grantham

Leo Cridland	157
Fenton Gregorich (8)	157
Phoebe Turner	158
Georgi-Lea Askew (9)	158
Bobby Gregorich	159
Tom Manning	159
Darwyn Temple (8)	160
Marcis Lilientals	160
Poppy Harding (8)	161
Lily Chivers (8)	161

Hattie Raeburn (8)	162
Leo Kavanagh	162
Vinnie McGregor Price (8)	163
Warren James Jackson (8)	163
James Martin (8)	164
George Crompton-Allan (8)	164
Lucy Hewitt	165
Jessica Marie Atkinson	165
Tegan Olivia Cameron (9)	166
Freddie Fowler (8)	166
Corey Bennett	167
Javan Mawu Elom Agboh (7)	167

The Phoenix School, Willburton

Mai Li	168
Deacon Jack Pattison (8)	168
Ellen Stewart (8)	169

The Poems

POETRY EMOTIONS - Eastern England

My Emotional Zoo

Be quiet you yellow, crazy kangaroo,
The sound of laughter as you bounce around,
You are the bubbly and crunchy excitement
In my emotional zoo.

Where are you when I need you?
You are a playful pink dog, with silky fur,
Babbling to me, 'Be happy and have some fun.'
You are the happiness in my emotional zoo.

Why are you always here?
You wild, purple monkey,
You scream with rage,
'Don't listen to happiness, fun is boring,' you tell me,
You are the anger in my emotional zoo.

How did you end up in my zoo?

You shy butterfly,
'Be careful,' you constantly stammer,
You sound like the leaves blowing away,
You are the prickly red fear in my emotional zoo.

Sometimes snoozing, sometimes screeching,
Never quiet,
Always awake,
A menagerie of emotions in this zoo.

And the zoo is me.

Alex Turnbull (10)
Archbishop Cranmer Academy, Nottingham

Beauty And The Beast

Anger, true anger,
A thunderstorm,
Roaring,
Stealing your soul,
People transformed.

Anger, true anger,
A lightning bolt,
Wicked, scary, loud,
Stabbing,
Hurting you.

Anger, true anger,
An alligator,
Definitely not purring,
Growling,
Waiting to devour you.

A volcano, exploding heads,
Shattering minds,
A true monster unleashed,
Tearing hearts, the Beast let loose!
But could you live without it?

Feelings,
Emotions,
Who I am,
Dancing, partying
Fighting, arguing,
Beauty and the Beast.

Joy, true joy,
A rainbow,
Singing,
Engulfing you with love,
People transformed.

Joy, true joy,
A cat,
Definitely not growling,
Purring,
Waiting to stroke you.

POETRY EMOTIONS - Eastern England

Joy, true joy,
A shooting star,
Inspiring, shiny, silent,
Hugging,
Loving you.

A sunbeam,
Mending heads, fixing minds, beauty let free,
Restoring hearts,
The wonder let loose, I cannot live without it.

Alexander Munn
Archbishop Cranmer Academy, Nottingham

Happiness To Me Is . . .

Happiness to me is
The aroma of warm, creamy chocolate
Perched on a glimmering bed of biscuits,
Like a tall, handsome soldier, guarding a castle.

Happiness to me is
The fizzy, tangy taste of sour lemons,
As my taste buds have a party.

Happiness to me is
The smell of my mum's perfume dancing under my nose,
Feeling safe and warm with my family.

Night after night I watched the dancing flames
In the fire putting me to sleep,
So I could dream my wildest dreams,
Content.

Happiness to me is
The warmth of the fire on a cold winter day,
Like a blanket of hope warming me up
As I eat a box of luxury chocolates, yum.
Content.

Sophie Rowe (8)
Archbishop Cranmer Academy, Nottingham

Emotions

Anger,
Anger hides in the depths of your heart,
Anger has ears like a steam train, a head as hot as fire,
Anger is an immense red cube punching you in the face with fury,
You are annoying, Anger.

Sadness,
Sadness lives in a damp, dark tunnel full of sad vibes,
Sadness has eyes like a sea, hair like seaweed,
Sadness destroys every speck of happiness inside me,
You are sorrowful, Sadness.

Happiness,
Happiness lives in a world of joy, laughter, hope, full of new beginnings
And everlasting endings,
Happiness has a smile like an upside-down rainbow,
A heart like candyfloss.
Happiness is love, hope, joy,
You are hope, you are life: Happiness.

Lucy Taylor (9)
Archbishop Cranmer Academy, Nottingham

Shy

My eyes are as black as ink,
My hair is glittery and very short,
Why when I'm shy, does it make me lie?
When I am shy I fall into a dream,
When I am shy I always giggle,
I am baby pink, maybe lighter,
Why when I'm shy do I turn rose-red?
My hair is glittery and very short,
Why do I always giggle and wriggle and turn when I am shy?
When I am shy why do I always speak quietly?

Molly Ashton (9)
Archbishop Cranmer Academy, Nottingham

Happiness

The taste, the sensation of popping candy tickling my mouth,
Making me want to hug the entire Earth every second.

The sound, the sweetness of a tweeting bird in the morning,
Making me dance with the spinning Earth every hour.

The aroma of the swirling perfect perfume,
Sweetening up my heart,
Reminding me of memories in the past,
Making me jump for joy.

The sense of the blasting beautiful fireworks leaping up,
With excitement, to the sky
Making me feel like I am exploding into one million pieces.

The feeling of a rainbow stretching out its peaceful colours,
Finding the treasure at the bottom,
Making me taste the clouds as yummy as candyfloss.

Mya Rose Edwards (10)
Archbishop Cranmer Academy, Nottingham

Hunger

A rumbling riot in my tummy,
What is going on in there?
Is it a volcano erupting?
A tsunami raging powerfully?
An earthquake perhaps bubbling and shaking in my tummy,
I look into an oven and a tremendous turkey is stood in there
Beside some tasty roast potatoes.

I am so hungry I hear the pudding whisper to me,
'Eat me! Eat me!'
I am as hungry as a wolf,
All I can think about is milk chocolate orange
And Mars bars, my favourite.
Hunger, a rumbling riot in my tummy.

Zac Hardy (8)
Archbishop Cranmer Academy, Nottingham

Determination – I Will

I will do it
I shall not quit
All I need is perfect persuasion
Feels like glitter, sparkles all night
What a wonderful sight
You appear just at the right moment
You are my determination!

You are as bright as the stars,
You give me advice,
You soothe me,
You are a diamond,
Pride.
I love that you're by my side,
You are my determination,
You coat me with determination!

Florence Olivia Sudborough (9)
Archbishop Cranmer Academy, Nottingham

Nervousness

You make me feel like a baby bird
Just about to fly for the first time
Reminding me of my first day at school.

You make me feel as grey as a dolphin
Flipping and flapping his flippers constantly,
Reminding me of dancing for the first time.

You make me feel as blue as the waves
Gushing against the wind viciously,
Reminding me of a spelling test.

You make me feel as sour as a lemon
Having a perfect party in my mouth,
Reminding me of a running race
Nervously standing in the cold, waiting for the word go.

Florrie Ryan
Archbishop Cranmer Academy, Nottingham

POETRY EMOTIONS - Eastern England

You Are . . .

You are as red as blood, but make me feel blue,
You make my heart bubble,
You build a brick wall around me,
I'm isolated, alone,
You are Sadness.

You are hurtful,
You push and punch me,
I'm angry, annoyed,
You are Sadness.

You are an echo,
You make my brain crunch,
You make me feel like I will never have a hand to hold,
I'm worried, heartbroken,
You are Sadness.

Frances Dodders
Archbishop Cranmer Academy, Nottingham

When And What I Fear

When I fear
Down my face comes a tear.
What I fear is when it's dark,
I hear owls hoot in the park.

When I fear
No one is near,
What I fear is the monsters that are under my bed,
So I never go underneath or they will bite off my head.

So fear is purple to me,
It makes me want a hot chocolate,
But I try to stay strong and bold,
It makes my heart go cold,
But Fear just zaps me with his laser eyes,
I want to ask him, 'You do this to me . . . why?'

Connie Storer (10)
Archbishop Cranmer Academy, Nottingham

When I'm Determined

When I'm determined
I kick a ball.
When I'm determined
I don't give up.
When I'm determined
I want to finish my work.
When I'm determined
The finish line is saying, 'Come on you will win.'

When I'm determined
I'm competitive.
When I'm determined
I want to win.
When I'm determined
I do all these things.

Charlie North
Archbishop Cranmer Academy, Nottingham

Happy

My beautiful baby sister,
Sleeping peacefully, brand new.

A summer's day, school holidays,
Birds singing their jolly song,
Knowing I will be outside all day.

Eating chocolate, feeling warm and cosy on a winter's night,
Content with my family,
All snug.

My favourite colour,
Turquoise -
All the thoughts make me feel
Happy!

Demi-Leigh Simpson
Archbishop Cranmer Academy, Nottingham

POETRY EMOTIONS - Eastern England

I Am Determined

Determination reassures me,
Determination is in the air,
Determination is in the oxygen,
Determined I am!

Determination makes me fly to the finish line,
Determination makes me run like I am in a rugby scrum,
Determination gives me wings
So I can soar.

Determination is me,
Determination is who I am,
Determination will always be with me,
Even if I'm sitting down!

Charlie Rains
Archbishop Cranmer Academy, Nottingham

Sadness

One man crying like a rainstorm thundering down,
Creating a long, thin, dull, grey river.

Sadness is being alone
On an old, dirty bench,
Strangers walk past,
Ignoring,
Like he is invisible.

A tin can clatters,
Rubbish at his feet,
Feeling hopeless.

That is Sadness.

Jessica Scott
Archbishop Cranmer Academy, Nottingham

I Was So Hungry

I was so hungry that
My tummy was roaring with starvation like a monster.

I was so hungry that
I felt like eating a bug that just waddled past me.

I was so hungry that
My tummy felt like an erupting volcano pouring out red-hot blood.

I was so hungry that
I felt like eating a whole Christmas dinner 10 times!

I was so relieved to see food,
I jumped up and down with joy.

Arthur Dexter
Archbishop Cranmer Academy, Nottingham

Joy!

Princess ponies in my dreams,
Princess ponies sing to me,
Princess ponies loving summer,
Princess ponies are like my mother,
Princess ponies are sweet and kind,
Princess ponies control my mind,
Princess ponies are wild and free,
Princess ponies are happy,
Princess ponies are as turquoise as can be,
Princess ponies protect me,
Princess ponies bring joy to me.

Serena Lee
Archbishop Cranmer Academy, Nottingham

POETRY EMOTIONS - Eastern England

The Best Day Of My Life

When I am happy
I play outside on a sunny day.
When I am happy
I open my birthday presents in May.
When I am happy
On Christmas Day I open my presents.
When I am happy
I play with friends on a school day.
But when I am happy
Will you be happy?

Sonny Towle
Archbishop Cranmer Academy, Nottingham

Sadness!

I am grey-blue,
A tear trickling down,
I am cold.
'Why are you here?' they say.
No one seems to care.
'I need a hug.'
'I want to play.'
Sadness covers me like a heavy coat,
'Please be kind,' I whispered.

Evie May Adu (9)
Archbishop Cranmer Academy, Nottingham

What Is Joy?

Joy is the whistling wind blowing my soft blanket
Through the window on a cold but sunny day,
I adore aroma of the roses in my garden,
The roses are as bright as the sun.

Joy sounds like someone saying, 'Hello,' in a soft but loud voice,
You are the colour yellow and the fun in my soul,
Joy feels like a lemon fizzing up in my mouth
And having a party.

Emily Wade
Archbishop Cranmer Academy, Nottingham

When I'm Angry

When I'm angry
I start to get in the Sea of Bother,
When I'm in the Sea of Bother
I erupt like a sultry volcano,
When I'm a sultry volcano
I fight like a wicked warrior killing everybody,
When I fight like a wicked warrior my taste buds
Burst like TNT blowing up.

Ethan Hose
Archbishop Cranmer Academy, Nottingham

POETRY EMOTIONS - Eastern England

Heartbroken

You are deep blue,
Silent, heavy, hurtful,
Roaring car engine falls silent,
The gushing, whistling, blowing of the wind falls still,
All is silent,
My heart is empty,
You are an unwelcome visitor,
Please go away.

Libby Kennedy
Archbishop Cranmer Academy, Nottingham

I Am Curious

I like to find out new things every day,
I am like a meerkat, sneaky,
I ignore everyone,
I am dark blue like a thunderstorm,
Curiosity grows in the depth of my stomach,
I smell like a burning brain overworking, ready to explode,
You keep me motivated,
I am curious!

Jenson Daubrah-Scott
Archbishop Cranmer Academy, Nottingham

A Puddle Of Tears

A puddle of tears wobbling like jelly in the wind.
A river of tears flowing down the mountainside.
A lake of tears sitting calmly on the bottom of the mountainside.
A sea of tears surrounding little England.
An ocean of tears isolating Europe.
A little boy sitting on his own at a new school,
Wobbling like a leaf in the wind.

Matthew Wyatt
Archbishop Cranmer Academy, Nottingham

Determination!

Determination, it keeps me going,
'Come on, you can't stop now,' it urges,
Determination turns me into Usain Bolt.

When I see the finish line it gives me a speed boost,
Determination makes me win every race,
Determination makes me sprout wings and fly,
Stick with me Determination, we make a great team!

Matthew Ward
Archbishop Cranmer Academy, Nottingham

Worried

When I am worried I'm silent.
When I am silent I'm anxious.
When I am anxious I'm scared.
When I am scared I'm terrified.
I just want to run away!

Joseph Hare-Goss
Archbishop Cranmer Academy, Nottingham

Anger

Anger, prepare for a daring ride,
Anger, fire rapidly burning inside,
Anger, always hurting your mind,
Anger, peace never comes inside,
Scream, scream, scream!

Anger, it's a speeding bullet,
Anger, you're in a sea of trouble,
Anger, count to ten, it's good advice,
Count to ten, you'll feel alright,
Anger, now you've left the daring ride.

Filip Majchrzak (11)
Boston St Mary's RC Primary School, Boston

Exciting Emotions

When you are hungry
You should be awake.
When you are hungry
Shout for some steak and cake!

When you are tired
You will need to
Rest your head
On your lovely, warm bed!

When you are sad
Sing your favourite song,
Then you will be glad!

When you are bored
Call the Lord.
When you are bored
Count your money
And see what you can afford,
It might be a doll or maybe a book,
But you might want a sword!

Charlotte Fowlston
Boston St Mary's RC Primary School, Boston

Birthday

B irthday presents I like, they bring such delight
I t's my birthday, let's celebrate, there's nothing to hate
R ound and round the party chairs, people are now sitting in pairs
T here's a buffet with lots of food, make sure you're not rude
'H appy birthday' everyone sings to me, I'm jumping happily
D ays and days I've been counting down, it's my birthday, no need to frown
A is for Aine which is amazing, when they said that it felt like my heart jumped out my chest
Y is for yeah, it's my birthday, I'm so happy.

Aine Larkin (10)
Boston St Mary's RC Primary School, Boston

POETRY EMOTIONS - Eastern England

What Emotion Am I?

I felt scared, I was all alone
As I turned my back I felt
There were monsters following me
I was all alone at home
Mum and Dad were gone for hours
I was starting to clench my fists
I was biting my nails as the clock was ticking by
My face went red as I got cross.

I was sweating
I was tingling
I was shaking
As I looked up at the midnight sky
I felt like I was being torn apart
I ran upstairs crying and pulling my hair
So I slammed the door
Then they came home
So I ran downstairs and was relieved and bursting with joy
And I almost turned into a fabulous, fantastic fish.

Carrianne Elisabeth Woods (10)
Boston St Mary's RC Primary School, Boston

Excited

Excited!
Excited is when you go with your friends somewhere.
Excited!
Excited is when I go to school.
Excited!
Excited is when I go swimming.
Excited!
Excited is when I go to parties.
Excited!
Excited is when I am with my family.
Emotions! Emotions! Emotions!

Maria Do Mar Albuquerque
Boston St Mary's RC Primary School, Boston

Emotion

H at on my head
A n ice cream in my hand
P laying games
P lanning parties for my birthday
Y ou with me

A flame goes around my body
N asty things I do
G ames I do not play
R ed means angry and that is me
Y ou need to see when I am angry

N ow they are ready for me
E veryone is looking at me
R emember to do your best
V ery nervous
O ver-shaking with fear
U nsure of what to do
S haking like mad.

Saida Sakalauskaite
Boston St Mary's RC Primary School, Boston

Disneyland Paris

I'm on the train to go to Disneyland, Paris,
Through the window I see the castle,
I feel happy.

I just got off the train running to the entrance
And I see everything like the parade, the fair, characters
And most of all the castle!
I feel happy.

Now the fireworks are starting,
The fireworks are going *boom, boom, boom,*
The crowd is cheering,
I feel happy.

Andreia Bark
Boston St Mary's RC Primary School, Boston

Emotions

E motions make you feel happy or sad
M adness makes you feel angry
O pen up to the world of emotions
T ime to get really joyful to the world
I mages of sad things make you cry
O pen up and take away your sadness
N ever turn away from happiness
S o you can spread joy to the world

A ngriness turns away from happiness
N ever does angriness turn to good emotions
G reat emotional power has anger
E motions never get real bad
R aging flames from River Rage

J umping up to excitement
O pening images of joy
Y ummy, yummy joyful food.

Ian Apilado
Boston St Mary's RC Primary School, Boston

Anger

There's one hot person lurking in your head,
No tears he will shed,
One little steam and he will come out,
He will kick, he will punch, he will shout.

Cool yourself down and don't talk,
Just eat a little slice of pork!
Singing out loud to save the joy,
Playing with your big teddy toy.

Just kiss Anger goodbye,
Go and have a rest, bye-bye.
He'll pop out of your head,
If you just go to bed.

Taniya Jiyo
Boston St Mary's RC Primary School, Boston

Emotions

E motions are like feelings
M aking decisions could make you angry
O pen your mind so then you can be full of joy in your heart
T ime to make a friend or else you will be sad
I magination is a dream, but it might be a nightmare and you will be full of fear
O n some occasions you are eating food that you don't like and that emotion is disgust
N ice stuff means excitement like it is your lucky day

J oy is in my heart every day
O pen hearts means excitement
Y ucky stuff means disgust

F oxes get scared pretty easily
E erie stuff means that you are freaking out
A pples make you happy
R ockets make you feel amazed.

Gabriel Vallido
Boston St Mary's RC Primary School, Boston

Do I Dare?

Do I dare pull her hair?
The energy bubbling up like a steaming potion.
Do I dare pull back her chair?
I'm so tempted, it's becoming an explosion.

Do I dare steal her teddy bear?
I am getting fuller to the second of emotion.
Do I dare push her down the stairs?
I can see it all in my head in slow motion.

Do I dare pretend not to care?
It is becoming a huge sensation.
Do I dare keep my share?
The emotion I'm writing about is called Temptation.

Hannah Sugg
Boston St Mary's RC Primary School, Boston

POETRY EMOTIONS - Eastern England

Poem Of Advice

Be brave
And you won't crave to see your family.

Don't be sad or you'll be bad
To see your friends run by.

If someone shall die
You'll surely cry and miss them so.

When you love
You feel like a dove.

Be happy
And you'll feel snappy.

Be silly
Just like Billy.

Have the sense
To not jump over the fence.

Esme Brown
Boston St Mary's RC Primary School, Boston

What Emotion Am I?

This poem is about emotions but with a twist,
It's a riddle, good luck.

I have wet hands, I feel like the ocean but with tears,
I feel like shouting and I feel like crying,
What emotion am I?
I am Sadness.

I feel happier and I feel like hugging everyone in the world,
I feel like a pot of gold,
What emotion am I?
I am Joy.

Well done, you've finished,
If you got them all right, well done.

Khim Stokes
Boston St Mary's RC Primary School, Boston

Mixed Emotions

When I am angry my face goes red.
When I'm tired I go to bed.
When I'm cold I need a hug.
When I'm sick I have a stomach bug.

When I'm happy I give a smile,
I'm bored in a line, it takes a while.
I'm nervous as I go on stage,
I'm stuck on my work, I've done hardly a page.

I'm lonely on my own,
Having fun on my phone.
My emotions are part of me,
Some are sad or fun you see.

Anger, tired, cold, sick, happy, bored,
Nervous, confused, lonely.

Danielle Gray
Boston St Mary's RC Primary School, Boston

Why Do You Want To Cry?

Laugh and relax, you've got to pay the tax.
All you want to do is cry, but look at all those smiles,
They're full of joy
And all you have to do is turn that frown upside down
And everything will be alright.

Look at the sky, it said, 'Goodbye,'
And all you do is cry.
You're full of gloom, it is your doom
And all you have to do is turn that frown upside down
And everything will be alright.
Please don't be sad, be glad,
Look at all the fun that can be had.
All you have to do is . . . smile.

Frazer Steadman (10)
Boston St Mary's RC Primary School, Boston

Waiting In Bed

Waiting in bed,
images of death and destruction
dancing in my head.
Losing family and friends,
zombies and skeletons,
So many different things
waiting in bed.
Wondering which way I'll go,
Better not be slow,
That spine-chilling thought.
Or if it will turn out different than I thought
And I will see everything again,
Everything except for that zombie,
That scared me to death,
Just waiting in bed.

Ethan Anthony Blakey (11)
Boston St Mary's RC Primary School, Boston

Anger

Anger is dark,
Anger is deep,
You can't recognise it in your sleep.

Anger is trouble,
Anger makes rubble,
Once you're angry, it's double the trouble!

Anger makes fights,
Anger makes dark lights,
Once you're in it, you're lost.

Anger is a roller coaster,
Anger is strife,
But Anger is in daily life.

Justin Jheo Cafe-Ebuen
Boston St Mary's RC Primary School, Boston

Mixed Emotions

Children are fine
When they are nine,
They are good as gold,
They are happy and never cold.

Everybody has emotions no matter what,
Everybody is happy when they get a hat.

  E is for excitement
  M is for melancholy
  O is for overjoyed
  T is for temper
  I is for impatience
  O is for over the moon
  N is for nervous
  S is for sympathy.

Abel Reji (9)
Boston St Mary's RC Primary School, Boston

Granny

I was sad . . .
When . . .
I heard my mum crying,
It was because my gran had died.

She went to India,
Me, my little sister
And my dad were alone at home,
We were so worried.

I was about to cry,
Granny was my gem,
We remember her as an angel that smiles,
I can't wait until I see her grave.

Joash Thomas (8)
Boston St Mary's RC Primary School, Boston

Untitled

I feel like an angry bull charging
The negative side of me unleashing,
My heart beating
Like a raged giant screaming,
Fire inside me crackling.

His eyes all fiery,
Seethe in your menacing look.
Your face stiff as a statue,
Bellowing, 'Why, why me?'
It has trapped me inside a steel cage,
No ice cools a heart of an angry man.
I feel like breathing fire.

Ziyad Rehan
Boston St Mary's RC Primary School, Boston

Anger

There's one little ghost lurking in your head,
No crocodile tears, just stress.
One little steam and *poof,* it's out,
It will pinch, push and one big kick in the back.

It will come very often, it's red with fire bursting off its head,
It steams a lot, it will fry your egg,
Just calm down, it will eventually die down.

Tomorrow it will come back
Anxiously bursting back into your head if you get messed.

Close your eyes, make a dream
And think about all the steam.

Sophie Hannah Brown (10)
Boston St Mary's RC Primary School, Boston

I Felt So Happy

I felt so happy,
When my mummy changed my nappy to keep me clean
So I am seen, the proudest person anyone will know,
I can let my great power show
And my best friend Louise who's a great fan of cheese
Said that she sees the beautiful trees
With lots of newborn and crusty leaves.
Later on I sang a song
And Louise said, it was a bit wrong!
But suddenly she asked me, 'How do you always get that smart look?'
And I said, 'Go to my home and read my 'fancy book'.'

Rico Bringeman
Boston St Mary's RC Primary School, Boston

A Flush Of Anger

First of all came the anger,
Me losing control, wanting to surrender.
Needing to stop but not having the power.
All of my anger bubbling up,
Here is my fist but now it's too much.

Seconds the sorrow is fulfilling my mind.
Now is the moment I'm giving up hope.
People laughing at me, people calling me names.
Feeling like trash, getting kicked all over the place.
Crying all night, crying all day,
Praying.

Mollie Jeanne Fitzgerald (10)
Boston St Mary's RC Primary School, Boston

Emotions, Emotions

First happy, then sad,
Emotions, emotions,
Sad again then mad!
Emotions, emotions,
Silly turns to crazy.
Emotions, emotions,
Next I feel determined.
Emotions, emotions,
Now I feel proud!
Emotions, emotions.

Grace Bartram
Boston St Mary's RC Primary School, Boston

Joy

Joy is a feeling,
Powerful and bright.

Joy is a feeling,
Loving and light.

Joy is a feeling,
Energetic and swift.

Joy is a feeling,
Caring and right.

Godwin Kozhukkullikkaran-Biji (8)
Boston St Mary's RC Primary School, Boston

Sadness Poem

Sadness got into my eyes
Like a stream of water tumbling down.
Whenever I cry, wherever I go,
It always seems to know.
Friends laughing, screaming,
Tears dropping, filling up into my heart.
Constantly crying all around,
Swishing like the trees and wind all around.
That's how Sadness got to me.

Angelika Kaczar
Boston St Mary's RC Primary School, Boston

When I Got Home From School

When I got home from school I saw
My sister eating Brussels sprouts,
My cat sat in a hot tub,
My dog eating soup,
My mum on TV (not very common),
My dad cooking (not that bad),
My baby cousin dancing (in a weird way)
And my aunt doing gymnastics . . .
When I ran upstairs I screamed, 'What is wrong with them today?'

Oliwia Banasiuk
Boston St Mary's RC Primary School, Boston

POETRY EMOTIONS - Eastern England

Hunger

Hunger is something you cannot stop,
You are hungry from ceiling to floor.
Pizza, hot dog, fries, you name it,
Whatever you are hungry for.

Mealtimes don't matter, you always want food,
You are hyper and crazy with glee.
When you eat there is a glow in your heart
And you don't need to pay a fee.

Oscar Gleeson-Garrard
Boston St Mary's RC Primary School, Boston

Anger

Anger is bad
So please calm down
But it won't stop.
It feels like a volcano erupting.
Anger feels like a building exploding.
Anger feels like a bomb exploding.
Anger feels like my world has broke into two.
Anger feels like my light has just gone out.

Anielis Kvedaravicius
Boston St Mary's RC Primary School, Boston

Scaredy Cat

I am so scared of everything
Apart from monsters.
Cats scare me.
Bats scare me.
Rats scare me.
Frogs scare me.
Dogs scare me.
But not monsters because they're scared of me.

Patryk Godzisz
Boston St Mary's RC Primary School, Boston

Burning, Fiery Anger

The emotion you feel, the anger consumed,
A plan to your brain goes boom!
A colossal pain goes lame,
Ugly monster in your brain.
The ancient monster passed away
Into your happiest dreams relieved,
I am calm and happy.
Now that monster will never appear again.

Brian Fernandes (11)
Boston St Mary's RC Primary School, Boston

POETRY EMOTIONS - Eastern England

What Emotion Am I?

Hiding under my blanket,
Closing my eyes,
I hear a noise,
What can it be?
A monster? A ghost?
I don't know!
My hands are tingling,
My head is sweating,
My skin is stretching.

What emotion am I?

I can feel my bed shaking,
Crying for mercy,
Just like me,
I'm alone,
In the dark,
In my head
Was a scary, big monster,
Under my bed.
My ears bending,
My mouth dropping,
My body shaking.

What emotion am I?

Mikayla Parangalan
Boston St Mary's RC Primary School, Boston

Tired

When I was tired
I went to sleep
I lay back down
But I heard a peep
I turned around
Because I was weak
And finally I got back to sleep.

Daniela Bringeman
Boston St Mary's RC Primary School, Boston

Love

Love is like the birds tweeting in the morning.
Love is like a bag of sweets exploding!
It's like you've seen a dozen hearts in the sky.
Love feels like you're flowing away and waving goodbye.
You will be very proud
When you see pink, fluffy clouds!
Love is like driving in a little car
And having a drink at the bar!

Alex Barsby (8)
Boston St Mary's RC Primary School, Boston

POETRY EMOTIONS - Eastern England

Happiness

Things that make me happy are . . .
Seeing Smudge in a nappy,
Going on holidays,
Having a meal,
Playing games,
Birthdays,
When I go to Grandma's and Grandad's house
That is what makes me happy.

Patrick McNally (8)
Boston St Mary's RC Primary School, Boston

Anger

Anger is like you breaking everything,
Surrounding you.
Anger is like a volcano exploding.
Anger tastes like extra hot peppers
And burnt spiders.
Anger is like a teacher giving
You the evil stare.

Louise Lerin Luck (9)
Boston St Mary's RC Primary School, Boston

Love

Love is like a sugary fairy.
Love smells like a romantic dinner.
Love is like a white, comfy cloud.
Love is as strong as a winner.
Love smells like golden perfume.
Love is like people kissing.
Love is like a pink cherry.
Love is like two people hugging together forever and ever.

Leon Przybylo
Boston St Mary's RC Primary School, Boston

Excited!

Excited is my favourite emotion.
Excited is in the morning and in the dark.
Excited lives in the ocean.

I like Excited because it lives in an alligator
And different places on the planet.

Excited is fun like being on a tractor
And feeling like a monster.

Patryk Cieslak (8)
Boston St Mary's RC Primary School, Boston

POETRY EMOTIONS - Eastern England

Love

Love is the first sight you will see.
She will be the white rose in your garden.
Every day she makes you laugh.
When you hug her she is your toasted marshmallow.
She will love you every day of the week or month.
You will have to love her as much as she does.
Together you are a candy heart that cannot be broken.

Jane Margaret Caldwell
Boston St Mary's RC Primary School, Boston

Ghouls

Tonight I would shake and the ground would quake of ghouls!
I would turn as white as a ghost
And think the coast is full of ghouls.
As a ghostly galleon, the size of a battalion
Howling past my room.
I stood as still as a hill thinking,
The ghouls are waiting to kill.

Godson Kozhukkullikkaran-Biji
Boston St Mary's RC Primary School, Boston

Confused

Being confused is when nobody listens.
Being confused is when nothing goes right
But sometimes being confused can help you not to go tight.
Being confused is when people call you crazy.
Being confused is when you can't think what to do
But being confused could be the best thing to happen to you
Because you learn from your mistakes.

Connor Blakey
Boston St Mary's RC Primary School, Boston

Emotions

E xcited is fun
X boxes are boring
C yprus is a good place, I feel happy there
I get very excited when I go dancing
T idying my room is boring
E xcited is always fun
D etect excitement easily.

Sophia Brigden
Boston St Mary's RC Primary School, Boston

POETRY EMOTIONS - Eastern England

Happy

Happy on a sunny day.
Happy playing with my friends.
Happy at my home.
Happy on a pink cloud.
Happy in space.
Happy in a tiny car.
Happy in my dreams.

Stefano Fiore
Boston St Mary's RC Primary School, Boston

Filip's Emotions

My eyes are sparkling,
My mouth is open,
My cheeks are red,
I am jumping up and down,
It is my birthday
And Dad has given me a new bike,
I am so very happy.

Filip Dlugolecki
Boston St Mary's RC Primary School, Boston

Loved

I love my mum.
I love my dad.
I love my sisters even though they're sometimes bad.
Love is like tweeting birds sitting in a tree
But Hate and Anger are something different.
It's like a volcano trying to erupt
And like fire in your arms.

Zuzanna Bogusz
Boston St Mary's RC Primary School, Boston

Anger

Anger – a fierce ball of fire.
Anger – hotter than an electric wire.
Anger – ominously lurking inside.
Anger – taking you for an uncontrollable ride.
Anger – crackling menacingly in the skin.
Anger – you'll just want to lock yourself in!

Joshua Mathews
Boston St Mary's RC Primary School, Boston

POETRY EMOTIONS - Eastern England

Emotions

A ngry is what I feel
N egative is what I am
G rumpy is how I am
E veryone is happy but I'm not
R aging is me.

Lilly Ireland
Boston St Mary's RC Primary School, Boston

Love!

Love is like a big, pink, fluffy bear cuddling you.
Love is like a yummy red chocolate heart
Melting inside of you.
Love is like smelly red and pink roses tickling you.
Love is when you are having a loving family around you.

Megan O'Connor
Boston St Mary's RC Primary School, Boston

Emotions

H is for happy when I got my Xbox 360
A is for amazed when I learnt to swim
P is for peace when I am alone
P is for precious memories that make me happy
Y is for your friends and family.

Finnley Danby (9)
Boston St Mary's RC Primary School, Boston

Mad

Mad feels like a temperature blowing up like a volcano.
Mad smells like totally melted ice cream from McDonald's.
Mad makes you want to wreck your Xbox 360.
Mad looks like burning lava.

Sasha/Aleksandrs Materevs (8)
Boston St Mary's RC Primary School, Boston

POETRY EMOTIONS - Eastern England

Pain

Pain is when an anvil falls on your heart.
Pain feels like metal spikes in your eyes.
Pain feels like being crushed by a trash compactor.
Pain feels like creepers exploding your brain.

Dawid Machnik
Boston St Mary's RC Primary School, Boston

Emotions

S adness is when I can't do my homework
A nger is when I fall out with Lukas
D isappointed is when I make my mum angry.

Igor Polakov
Boston St Mary's RC Primary School, Boston

Feeling Overdramatic

Feeling overdramatic is when I find a ginormous, monstrous spider in the house,
Feeling overdramatic is like acting Shakespeare in a tremendous play,
Feeling overdramatic is when a desperate balloon just popped.

Feeling overdramatic is like finding out you left your golden sparkling Labrador at home for 'bring your pets to school' day.
Feeling overdramatic is when you go to school in your bunny rabbit pyjamas because you left your uniform at home.
Feeling overdramatic is like eating a blazing, spicy, boiling hot chilli.

Feeling overdramatic is like looking into the sky while World War Two is going on,
Feeling overdramatic is when you're in a fight with your favourite pop star, Ariana Grande,
Feeling overdramatic is going crazy, eating too much sugar.

Matilda Lockton (8)
Christ The King RC Primary School, Leicester

Joy Is?

Joy is playing hockey,
Joy is buying new football boots,
Joy is as warm as the sun.

Joy is as sweet as candyfloss,
Joy is as sparkly as glitter,
Joy is something that never ends.

Joy is like seeing your cousin for the first time,
Joy is like eating steak,
Joy is like playing video games.

Joy is like sweets and candy,
Joy is like eating chocolate,
Joy is as sweet as strawberries.

Zach Woolley (8)
Christ The King RC Primary School, Leicester

POETRY EMOTIONS - Eastern England

Surprised Is . . .

Surprise is finding out your netball team won the tournament
And you hold the trophy.
Surprise is going downstairs at Christmas
And when you go into the living room there is an avalanche of presents.
Surprise is getting something you want on your birthday.

Surprise is when I get a surprise party.
Surprise is as colossal as a titan.
Surprise is realising you're going on holiday to Florida.

Surprise is like bees getting lots of honey.
Surprise is getting a scrumptious dinner.
Surprise is getting a new baby.

Darryl Reyes (8)
Christ The King RC Primary School, Leicester

Love Is . . .

Love is a glistening moon that is glimmering,
and shining in the night,
Love is like a bright crimson rose that never dies,
Love is a midnight-black horse galloping free with its owner.

Love is like a pearl-white, fuzzy cloud in the shape of an elegant heart,
Love is as colourful as shining, rainbow fireworks,
Love is a brave dog with a bone in the wild.

Love is like a piece of sugar-brown, delectable, delicious piece of chocolate,
Love is like a tiny ginger kitten helping its sibling,
Love is a beautiful, loving heart pounding for someone else's heart.

Verity Havenhand (8)
Christ The King RC Primary School, Leicester

When Cheerfulness Strikes

Cheerfulness is playing with the people you adore,
Cheerfulness is as sweet as cane sugar,
Cheerfulness is a warm fuzzy feeling inside.

Cheerfulness is seeing a person for the first time,
Cheerfulness is as sweet as making new friends,
Cheerfulness is being a cheerleader.

Cheerfulness is like a turtle on a tropical island,
Cheerfulness is the opposite to sour sadness,
Cheerfulness is as bright and bouncy as a puppy in the glimmering sun.

Cheerfulness is the fuel to Heaven!

Maya Joseph-Casas (8)
Christ The King RC Primary School, Leicester

Bliss

Blissful is when you bite into mouth-watering chocolate,
Blissful is like you're in a relaxing, bubbly, boiling hot tub,
Blissful is a sandy paradise with beautiful, clear water.

Blissful is watching twinkling stars at night,
Blissful is seeing candlelight glowing in a dark room,
Blissful is hearing a bird's graceful call in the morning.

Blissful is a comfy bed that you sink into,
Blissful is a peaceful place that you get snug as a bug in,
Blissful is like you've been taken to a stress-free planet
Alone with everything just . . . perfect!

Evie Wenlock
Christ The King RC Primary School, Leicester

POETRY EMOTIONS - Eastern England

Disgust Is . . .

Disgust is seeing tarantula skin,
Disgust is eating mouldy broccoli,
Disgust is smelling burnt toast.

Disgust is being forced to eat lime-coloured mushrooms
And out-of-date Brussels sprouts,
Disgust is playing with Barbie dolls with messy hair,
Disgust is having sticky, slimy honey poured on your head.

Disgust is not having a shower or a bath for a week,
Disgust is as disgusting as oozing chickenpox,
Disgust is a blue, rotten banana.

Amber Bartholomew
Christ The King RC Primary School, Leicester

Ferocious Is . . .

Ferocious is taking a bone off a vicious dog,
Ferocious is an exploding sun,
Ferocious is eating an onion with its skin.

Ferocious is swallowing a ghost chilli without milk or water,
Ferocious is when you find out your friend is lying,
Ferocious is when your majestic Xbox breaks.

Ferocious is an angry cheetah,
Ferocious is when you're in the middle of something
And your mum tells you to stop.
Ferocious is eating a cat's fish.

Braydon Andrea Contina (8)
Christ The King RC Primary School, Leicester

Love Is . . .

Love is a gorgeous flower that never withers,
Love is like watching fireworks exploding into various different shapes,
Love is a powerful word that can reach your heart.

Love is beautiful memories when you are married,
Love is a box of yummy Guylian chocolates,
Love is like a glimmering star that never stops twinkling.

Love is as sweet as candyfloss,
Love is like a bright rainbow that never ends,
Love is a shy shadow that never disappears.

Jaime John (8)
Christ The King RC Primary School, Leicester

Excitement Is . . .

Excitement is when I found out my mum was having a baby boy!
Excitement is when I smile like I am ready to burst with joy!
Excitement is like when I get a brand new toy!

Excitement is watching the stars twinkling in the sky,
Excitement is a mist of joy . . . but why can we not have more?
Excitement is not knowing something but then finding out.

Excitement is as sweet as sugar.
Excitement is a firework bright and colourful.
Excitement is as bright as the sun . . .

Sharndre Garrity (9)
Christ The King RC Primary School, Leicester

POETRY EMOTIONS - Eastern England

Fazbear's Fright

Fear is being at Freddy Fazbear's pizzeria,
Fear is watching a blazing comet coming down to Earth,
Fear is watching a giant meteorite burning up in the sky.

Fear is watching the largest nuclear bomb exploding,
Fear is being trapped in a ring of fire,
Fear is as horrid as Horrid Henry.

Fear is hearing about the terrorists in France,
Fear is getting bullied by people tougher than you,
Fear is having your best friend taken away from you.

Felix Kennedy (8)
Christ The King RC Primary School, Leicester

Excitement Is . . .

Going on an exciting holiday,
Finding out you're getting a special surprise,
Going out to a concert.

Seeing someone for the first time,
Watching fireworks sparkle in the sky
While stars fly by.

Watching your favourite movie,
Getting a new game for your birthday,
When new memories occur excitement is what you're looking for.

Luke Gibson (9)
Christ The King RC Primary School, Leicester

Nervous

Nervous is getting butterflies in my tummy.
Nervous is your heart beating fast.
Nervous is getting hot and sweaty.

Nervous is getting anxious about the audience.
Nervous is worrying if it will go well.
Nervous is getting frightened about the noise.

Nervous is getting pins and needles.
Nervous is trying to be brave.
Nervous is trying to forget about it.

Hannah Grace Michaluk (9)
Christ The King RC Primary School, Leicester

A Page Of Fear

Fear is like going to the top of a towering roller coaster,
Fear is like hiking up a colossal mountain,
Fear is like playing scary games that give you nightmares.

Fear is like getting a disturbing nightmare,
Fear is like having the lights out,
Fear is like destroying a vase and keeping it a secret.

Fear is like being sent to the headmaster's office,
Fear is like failing a test,
Fear is like going to school for the first time.

Steven Darko
Christ The King RC Primary School, Leicester

POETRY EMOTIONS - Eastern England

When Anger Returns

Anger is when your brother is teasing you.
Anger is like a mad bull.
Anger is like your body turning into a robot that is uprising.

Anger is like a great white shark.
Anger is when you're like a drunk man with a gun shooting people.
Anger is like a lion that has not eaten for 10 weeks free from its cage.

Anger is when your head turns red, full of anger.
Anger is as red as a tiger.
Anger is like a fearsome robot.

Benedict Mathew
Christ The King RC Primary School, Leicester

Fear Is . . .

Fear is finding out you have a massive spider on your bed,
Fear is having an active volcano near your house,
Fear is having a horrifying nightmare.

Fear is losing your loving family,
Fear is having a hurricane in Leicester,
Fear is having a poisonous snake.

Fear is getting braces,
Fear is as frightening as breaking your bones really painfully,
Fear is riding a two wheel bike for the first time.

Tara Lacar
Christ The King RC Primary School, Leicester

Jolly Is . . .

Jolly is finding out your adorable, cute newborn baby cousin is born.
Jolly is when you go to the incredible India.
Jolly is when you have fun playing with your sisters.

Jolly is watching the ending of a fabulous movie.
Jolly is like showing your class an amazing role play.
Jolly is as good as eating a delicious ice cream.

Jolly is like meeting Santa for the first time.
Jolly is as proud as winning a competition.
Jolly is something that will never stop!

Hannah Philip
Christ The King RC Primary School, Leicester

Things That Make Me Furious

Furious is being bossed around.
Furious is having to listen to moaning.
Furious is not getting the things you want.

Furious is listening to boring talking.
Furious is being told rules again and again.
Furious is an exploding bomb.

Furious is like someone thinking they are better.
Furious is as flaming as a volcano.
Furious is as red as the reddest tomato.

Karolina Mocko
Christ The King RC Primary School, Leicester

POETRY EMOTIONS - Eastern England

Cheerful!

Cheerful is like getting a wonderful, adorable pet.
Cheerful is when someone makes you feel better.
Cheerful is when your mum makes delicious cupcakes.

Cheerful is as sweet as cola liquorice.
Cheerful is as happy as bursting love.
Cheerful is like jumping with exciting feelings.

Cheerful is like bursting with joy.
Cheerful is as exciting as getting a surprise birthday party.
Cheerful is as hot as the sun.

Lana Wood (9)
Christ The King RC Primary School, Leicester

Fear Is . . .

Fear is waking up to a bad dream.
Fear is finding a hairy spider in your bedroom.
Fear is when your friend jumps out at you.

Fear is going on a roller coaster for the first time.
Fear is having an injection that really hurts.
Fear is believing in vampires.

Fear is seeing a ferocious tiger.
Fear is as terrifying as a loud bang of a volcano erupting.
Fear is like watching a war.

Alice Wakely (8)
Christ The King RC Primary School, Leicester

The Art Of Hatred

Hatred is a stroll in the park of war,
Hatred is like needing your enemies to bring an end to the world,
Hatred is too much low self-esteem.

Hatred is when your face turns red with rage,
Hatred is getting revenge,
Hatred is a horrible feeling that comes naturally.

Hatred is happiness, on an opposite day!
Hatred is doing evil in the hope that no good comes from it.
Hatred is a source that gives a power to contain our secrets.

Isaac Harry Warren (9)
Christ The King RC Primary School, Leicester

Joyfulness Is . . .

Joyfulness is spending time on my own.
Joyfulness is finding I am having a birthday party on my birthday.
Joyfulness is playing spies with my sister.
Joyfulness is dancing gracefully.
Joyfulness is finding a fluffy cloud.
Joyfulness is finding out that it is Christmas Day.
Joyfulness is seeing someone you haven't seen before
Or going somewhere you haven't gone before.
Joyfulness is entering a competition you haven't entered before.

Leona Boby (8)
Christ The King RC Primary School, Leicester

POETRY EMOTIONS - Eastern England

Fear

Fear is like being trapped in a damp, wet maze,
Fear is a fearsome dragon destroying the Earth,
Fear is an unstoppable black hole tearing the Earth to pieces.

Fear is an eyebrow-raising black widow about to strike,
Fear is watching a massive tornado come towards your house,
Fear is watching a huge nuclear bomb explode.

Fear is working at war,
Fear is losing your mum or dad,
Fear is a soaking flood flooding your house.

Fear is watching a scary horror movie,
Fear is thinking of being dead,
Fear is being trapped in a room of spiders.

Fear is being beaten at a game so you lose your winning streak,
Fear is about to go in front of 10,000 cheering fans,
Fear is being unwanted.

Joshua Botterill (8)
Christ The King RC Primary School, Leicester

Untitled

Suddenly quiet,
Help!
You're caught, you will be shot.
Murmuring, crying,
War, it was all real.

Hetty Life
Coltishall Primary School, Norwich

Untitled

I can feel the cold air touching my face.
I can feel enormous pressure,
I can feel fire, I can feel anger,
I can feel rage building up deep inside, deep inside,
Deep inside feeling like it's going to blow,
Going to blow, going to blow.
I try to keep it in but I can't take it anymore,
The volcano inside me is about to erupt, to erupt, to erupt.
Tremor waves crash onto the shore,
Onto the shore, onto the shore.
Big black clouds with bolts of lightning form,
Lightning form, lightning form.
The river of emotions is about to reach the sea, the sea, the sea.
Lava flowing off it, lava flowing off it, lava flowing off it,
Clouds of sulphur surrounding it,
Like a tiger about to pounce,
Like an owl about to dive, about to dive,
About to dive when I feel nothing can stop me,
I hear a voice, 'It's okay.'

Kenneth Frost
Coltishall Primary School, Norwich

Depression

Depression is happiness dying, bullying, anger, awful.
Alone as a lone wolf.
Depression is a black cloud hanging over you!
Depression sucks!

Depression is happiness dying.
Depression is happiness dying.
Sad, crying,
Alone, darkness.
Torture, mean despair,
Depression, abandoned.

Noah Christian Smith
Coltishall Primary School, Norwich

POETRY EMOTIONS - Eastern England

Anger

My pot has boiled over,
The time has come,
I've got a feeling in my body,
Or either a prickle in my thumb.

My heart turns to a high level of annoyance,
A ball of fire turns me neon red,
I'm irritated at someone,
There's fury in my head.

Suddenly a devil comes out to play,
Then there was a different feeling,
The scared children ran away.

As a clown begins to scare,
I'm in pure silence,
While the child holds their wounded teddy bear,
Don't mess with me my friend,
Or your life will come to an end.

Grace Baynes (10)
Coltishall Primary School, Norwich

The Smiling Skeleton

Gazing around,
He'd lost some of its magic and sparkle no longer shone.
Gone missing.
What has happened?
Why?
He didn't much like the sound of any of this.
Argue, even fight,
Caught up in
Violent arguments,
Motionless, wicked, twisted, distorted.
Fate?
Skeleton.

George Parkerson
Coltishall Primary School, Norwich

My Frustration

Hands clasped together so tightly, like never before.
I am the waterfall dripping off your young faces.
Trying to turn your frown upside down
Is like trying to avoid chocolate forever.
Migraines keep on coming one after another.
I am touching and constantly looking for something to do,
But there's nothing.
Angrily trying to sing a solo,
To forget all of me.
I am looking in the mirror thinking, *who have I become?*
People are slowly telling me to calm down
And take deep breaths, but it's no use.
My teeth are tapping together,
As tight as my shoe laces.
I am slowly but surely becoming something else.

Honey Beatrice Rotchell (10)
Coltishall Primary School, Norwich

Anger

Anger is a red ball of despair,
Floating in the open air,
Making everyone hate, hate, hate,
A feeling with the biggest weight,
A weight of fury and being scary,
Anger is big and hairy,
Jumping out when you least expect it,
Once he's out you'll have a fit,
Screaming, crying, shouting loudly,
If he's out you won't be cowardly,
You'll go crazy, you'll break a limb,
So everyone watch out for him!

Max Westmorland
Coltishall Primary School, Norwich

POETRY EMOTIONS - Eastern England

Depression Hurt

Like a dark figure lurking in the shadows.
A cloud as black and empty as my wicked heart looms over the silent Earth.
Depression is a death-eater consuming all of the people's happiness in one breath.
The cold is eating away their gloomy faces,
Allowing the ice-cold touch of depression to enter their hearts.
Depression hurts.
From the dark cloud, Anger spikes no control over who it will hit.
No control over the strength of the lightning bolt,
Which is coming towards you.

Oz Kemp
Coltishall Primary School, Norwich

Guilty . . .

When I am guilty, I am friendless and paralysed
Holding in my solemnity
I feel empty
But somewhat disposed of hope
I don't want to feel filthy.

Pitiful cannot describe me,
Rivalled really not,
Affliction of guilt, I don't think so,
Awakeness makes me feel like I'm going to rot!
Worse is the only thing which grows within.

Lucy Papworth
Coltishall Primary School, Norwich

Anger

Hate building up inside me.
I try to ignore it but I can't.
My brain starts to boil.
My hand clutches into a fist.
My teeth are bared.
I am not still anywhere.
I am running, running at speed,
Running at my target,
Who also happens to be running, running at speed,
Running from its predator.

James Marshall (10)
Coltishall Primary School, Norwich

Anger

I'm a volcano about to erupt and explode,
I shout, shout, shout!
Wanting it to stop, it's too much,
Trying to breathe, it won't stop.
How can it?
Mum's shouting in one ear,
'Come down for tea, now!'
And Dad shouting in the other ear,
'Come and help me with the car!'
How can I? How can I? How can I?

Sophia Stevens
Coltishall Primary School, Norwich

POETRY EMOTIONS - Eastern England

Anger

He was stamping his feet,
His face was bright red,
He was a volcano about to explode,
Screaming at the top of his lungs,
He was ripping his hair, almost pulling it off,
His mum as eager as a puppy
Trying to find out what all the fuss was about,
He counted to ten to calm himself down,
1, 2, 3, 4, 5, 6, 7, 8, 9,
'Argh!' he screamed.

Ayten Kazemaliloo
Coltishall Primary School, Norwich

Being Lost

A ball of red fire,
Mixed into the flames of Hell.
A drop of water
In amongst the ocean.
A tiny grain of sand,
Not knowing its name within the walls of the beach.
A spot of black,
In with the ever darker universe.
A street, lost in all the others there.

Ellie Loiez
Coltishall Primary School, Norwich

Anger

My frustration is like a car.
It's driving me over the edge.
I can't control myself any more.
My head is spinning around.
I've gone into 6th gear,
There's no more happiness . . .
Left in my engine.
Will this angry road trip ever end?

Charlie Jones
Coltishall Primary School, Norwich

My Abandonment Poem

I am like a World War Two bomb,
Solitary as I fall from the plane,
Then years later shunned,
As no one knows if I will explode.
I am like a dog with no energy,
So downhearted.
I am like the last puppy in a litter,
All abandoned and left out.

Leo Pearce
Coltishall Primary School, Norwich

Cold Revenge

Like a tiger hunting its prey.
As icy as a cold night.
I feel someone is plotting a plan.
Angry, annoyed and hurt,
Wanting to get them back.
As frosty as ice melting on your hand,
I feel more hate.

Annabel Jameson
Coltishall Primary School, Norwich

Jealousy

Staring intently at the thing you want most.
Angry with the thing you receive.
The sports team tryouts are over
And didn't get in.
Feeling like you are the odd one out.
Everyone gets what they want except you.
Feeling like you should run away
And never return!

Harrison Brooks
Coltishall Primary School, Norwich

Ride Of Happiness

As happy as a panting dog.
As joyful as first place in a marathon.
As exhausted as a gold medallist in the Olympics.
As happy as a mother with a newborn baby.
As content as a football team winning the FA Cup.
As merry as a boy getting what he wanted for Christmas.

Toby Spalding (9)
Coltishall Primary School, Norwich

Love

Love is a blooming flower,
Love is so warm and bright.
Love is when you find the one who's right for you.
Love, love everywhere,
Keep looking till you find your pair.

Daisy Lewin
Coltishall Primary School, Norwich

POETRY EMOTIONS - Eastern England

I Remember

I remember, I remember
When I was young
All the nice songs I sang
With my cousins and I
We used to play around and fly.

I remember, I remember
The things I used to play
Singing and clapping all throughout the day
And when my kittens got a bit cheeky
I would go next to them and be sneaky.

I remember, I remember
When I was little
All the hidden snacks I used to nibble.

I remember, I remember
The programme I watched every night
Oh! What a beautiful sight!
When will I catch a flight
To go to that amazing sight?

The sight that I remember!

Maryam Sageer (9)
Fig Tree Primary School, Nottingham

Yummy For My Tummy

When I see food,
I am in a mood.
When I am hungry
I need a bakery.
Sometimes when I am crazy,
I need a salty lolly.
When I see a kitchen,
I feel like eating a chicken.
When I see an eating pan,
I feel like a pan.
Please do not give me a dummy.
Rather give me something to put in my tummy.
I need noodles,
But I don't want to wear my doodles.
I like a chocolate bar,
But I am not keen for a shooting star.
I like meat,
But I don't like the heat.
Give me a pot,
So I can have some apricot.
I'm ready to go to the kitchen,
Not very eager for fiction.
Reading my poem
You can tell I'm hungry.
So give me something yummy,
I would love this yummy to go in my tummy.

Mustafa Siraj Uddin Hussain (8)
Fig Tree Primary School, Nottingham

POETRY EMOTIONS - Eastern England

I'm So Excited

My heart masticates a million veins
Putting pressure to its peak;
Cracking from one ear to another
Passionately to meet you here.
Lifted up inside,
Eyes and mouths widely
Dreaming about you.
Few more minutes
And you will be mine.
I'm really hoping,
Wondering,
Dreaming
And screaming for you.
After a long time my dream
Will come true.
I am in the city centre
To get you.
I am so excited as I am
Going to the shop.
I am asking the lady
If you are in stock.
She said, 'Yes,'
So I am buying you.

I love you, my Samsung Galaxy,
You are mine forever.

Haaris Minhas (8)
Fig Tree Primary School, Nottingham

I Can't Wait

I'm ready
I'm so glad
Lunch is waiting to be had.
I'm so hungry;
Looking for my food
I am desperate
I'm in the mood.
I can't wait
One second more.
I will eat your lunch
As I'm reaching before
But I don't want
You to hurt
I don't want to be known
Known as disconcert
Be my friend and let's share
And there is no erring
My mummy told me
Sharing is caring.

Maria Zainab (7)
Fig Tree Primary School, Nottingham

POETRY EMOTIONS - Eastern England

A World Free Of Homework

Every Friday
I receive my homework
My Miss wants us
To bring it back
Before next Friday
Whenever I sit down
To finish this monster
My favourite cartoons starts showing off
My baby sister feels she needs to scream
My dad brings home something exciting
But
My mum insists on me finishing my homework
I think she's always in the plan against me
I hate my homework
It takes my happiness away
Life is hard
So is the homework
I want this world
So free of homework.

Izaan Khan
Fig Tree Primary School, Nottingham

Football Mania

Football is cool.
It is a kind of duel.

I always save a goal.
I act quickly like fire control.

The World Cup is here.
I am ready to greet and cheer.

My favourite team is in.
I feel for them like a conjoined twin.

The entire world is buzzing.
They are thunderous as they care for nothing.

The crowd is cheering
And has begun shouting.

Hooray for the winners,
Hope tonight they will have mouth-watering dinners.

Mohammad Isa Shahid (8)
Fig Tree Primary School, Nottingham

When I First Felt Love

When I was born I felt love.
She gave me a name
Like I was the aspartame.
Her hugs were warm like a teddy
So I hugged her as I was ready.
Then she gave me a kiss.
Then I gave her a bite.
I wasn't sleeping
And my mum yawned and yawned.
So that's my story when I was born.
Mums are blessings and that's true!
Mum, you're the best and I love you!

Zaynab Binte Haider (8)
Fig Tree Primary School, Nottingham

POETRY EMOTIONS - Eastern England

She Smiled At Me

My mum smiles at me in a good mood.
I say to her, 'I want some food.'

Whenever I want a huggy,
She gives me a special huggy called Buggy.

I'm really grateful to her for always being there,
Me and her work as a pair.

I kiss her goodnight,
I know she guarded that as a knight.

I love you lots and lots my mummy,
You are the best and soothe me like a dummy.

Though sometimes I am naughty when you've got lots to do,
You become grumpy but I know you love me too.

Noor-Ul-Ain Ahmed (8)
Fig Tree Primary School, Nottingham

Me And Her

I have a lovely, beautiful sister.
She called me a mister.

Her hair spins when she plays.
She pretends that she is a pony when she is a blaze.

She always gives me a big kiss.
I really love her, she is my big sis.

We have a friendship that I thought we chased.
I am like spaghetti and she is my tomato paste.

I feel delighted when she makes me food.
She is my best friend and I am her dude.

She says to me that we will be best friends forever.
I am very fond of her whatsoever.

Ruqqaya Karam-Noor Shiekh (8)
Fig Tree Primary School, Nottingham

Me And My Brother

When I am sad
He makes me mad
If I am upset
He teases me by calling Juliet
When I am singing
He thinks Pavlov bells are ringing
If we are playing cricket
He is pleased to have my wicket
I feel my brother is annoying
His nature is destroying
Whatever he does anyway
I love to celebrate his birthday
I know he loves me . . . deep in his heart
I do love him . . . my brother is smart.

Daniyal Imran (7)
Fig Tree Primary School, Nottingham

When My Mum Is Sad, I'm Sad Too

When my mum is sad
I feel really bad.

When this new baby boy cries
I think I should get him toys.

If he is not well
I try not to yell.

He is my brother
He cries a lot to my mother.

I wish I had a magic wand to transmit healing vibes
So he won't tease my mum and have his medicine prescribes.

Muneer Raza (8)
Fig Tree Primary School, Nottingham

POETRY EMOTIONS - Eastern England

Happy Hippo

The jungle is all happy
There's laughter all around,
Except down by the river
Where there's no fun to be found.

The chimpanzees are loopy
Chattering with glee
And when no one is watching
They chomp upon a flea.

They spot a hippo in a swamp
Acting in a mood
They laugh and point
Saying he's a grump and being rather rude.

The chimps ask what's up
Giggling occasionally,
The hippo says so glum,
'I don't know what's wrong with me.'

He says, 'No one ever listens
My jokes are just a bore
I'm so full of doom and gloom
No one likes me any more!'

'I wish I could be like a lion,
So brave and so strong,
Or like you chimps
Having a laugh and always getting along.'

A chimp says, 'Be more confident
They'll soon see and then
They'll know your jokes are funny
And you'll all be friends again.'

The jungle is all happy
There's laughter all around
And if you go down to the river
There's a happy hippo to be found.

Rose Hardiman
Harby CE Primary School, Melton Mowbray

Help Me

On the dark street,
There's an ordinary house,
With an ordinary family,
That the curse of the witches lies upon,
The eyes of the witches lie in the breeze,
The mouth whispers in the bedroom,
The ears hear in the attic,
The hand clenches in the cupboard,
The nose smells blood in the kitchen,
The hair tangled in the floorboards,
Ready to twine up your leg,
But here's the scare,
The one line you should beware,
The stairs creak,
As you climb them with your feet,
The bathroom door chirps as you twist the handle,
You perch your toes upon the toilet floor,
You hear the click of the door,
When you hear that terrifying sound,
You suddenly know you'll never get out,
As the old mirror shines,
All the features . . .
The witches' eyes . . .
Now I'll tell you which house the curse lies upon,
3, 2, 1 . . . you're gone.

Aisling Eliza Giltinan (10)
Harby CE Primary School, Melton Mowbray

POETRY EMOTIONS - Eastern England

Sorrow From Your Heart

If you think deep and hard,
You can feel the past sadness,
It fills you with sorrow, pain of a faraway love,
Nightmares can haunt you of horrible times,
A thing like this sadness does not let you forget,
But that is its job.

If you think deep and hard,
Memories of friends falling out come back,
Your favourite person can be lost long ago,
The time you couldn't do anything you loved,
A thing like this sadness does not let you forget,
But that is its job.

If you think deep and hard,
You remember when unbearable thoughts ruled your mind,
When you could not deal with your emotions
And when you realised sorrow is in your heart,
A thing like this sadness does not let you forget,
For a good reason because that is its job.

Millie May Jessica Coles
Harby CE Primary School, Melton Mowbray

My Emotions

My emotion is happy, it's coming to me,
Please don't remove that feeling from my body!

My emotion is sad, it's storming over me,
Please don't let that be, I want to be free!

My emotion is angry, it's hunting me,
Please calm down, don't let that be!

My emotion is excited, it's jumping over me!
I can't stop smiling, as I am really happy.

My emotion is upset, please stop this from me!
Don't let me be upset, don't let that be!

My emotion is crazy, I just can't stop!
Please don't remove it, it's just too funny!

Thomas Bosley
Harby CE Primary School, Melton Mowbray

My Dream

My dream is to be a dancer,
So I can move to the music,
Flying through the air,
My dream,
Feeling happy, feeling free,
Giving peace to the world,
Giving peace to me,
My dream,
Having to perform,
Having an audience,
Having a lifetime to remember,
My dream.

Lola Sealey (10)
Harby CE Primary School, Melton Mowbray

POETRY EMOTIONS - Eastern England

The Fear

I feel a shiver up my spine,
I tell myself I'll be just fine.

Spider crawling,
Bone snap,
Clown snigger,
Big gap.

A needle sticks into my arm,
It fills my body with alarm.

Spider crawling,
Bone snap,
Clown snigger,
Big gap.

Everything turns midnight-black,
'Help!' I shout, there's no answer back . . .

Olivia Sian Martin (10)
Hasland Junior School, Chesterfield

Big Warm Smile

A big warm smile I had today
Because I met some new friends yesterday.
A big warm smile I have here
Because I can remember all the wonderful holidays I had last year.
A big warm smile I had
Because I have an amazing, wonderful, funny dad.
It's great to have an amazing smile
Because it makes me feel on top of the pile.

Hannah Jeanie Smithson (11)
Hasland Junior School, Chesterfield

Happiness

Yay! It's my birthday
I have cake
And a snake
Just a baby milksnake
A new football kit
(Norwich City's home kit!)
I'm going to Pleasurewood Hills
With my friends
We can go on Wipeout
Screaming at the sharp bends
Hobbs Pit might be scary
But it's actually a laugh.

All this makes me happy
Makes me fill up with joy
Ecstatic, fun, over the moon
The feeling like I'm in a hot-air balloon.

Having big midnight feasts
FIFA tournaments
Where I never win
Going out to the park
Our bike bells go *ting!*
Playing rounds of manhunt
Climbing up trees
We see a dead bird with
Some type of disease.

All this makes me happy
Makes me fill up with joy
Ecstatic, fun, over the moon
The feeling like I'm in a hot-air balloon.

Amazing, awesome
Wonderful places
Sitting in the sun
Getting a deep brown tan
Every morning I wake up
And go to the pool
Food from the shops in the resort
Exotic fruit of every sort

POETRY EMOTIONS - Eastern England

Renting bikes
Racing round, really fast
You might even see Lamborghinis go past.

All this makes me happy
Makes me fill up with joy
Ecstatic, fun, over the moon
The feeling like I'm in a hot-air balloon.

Alex Smith (11)
Hethersett VC Junior School, Norwich

Temper! Temper!

I told you to stop!
It was all because of you,
You're getting on my wick,
The clock is ticking,
My temper's ascending.

You get on my nerves,
I know these stupid words,
Listen to my advice,
It's annoyance right?

When your parents say no!
When you just wanna have it,
You slam the door,
Go to your room.

You get on my wick,
I know these stupid words,
Listen to my advice,
It's annoyance right?

Face like fire,
Fluttery fairies,
Face like fire,
Fluttery fairies,
Now listen to my advice
It's annoyance right?

Millie Bambridge
Hethersett VC Junior School, Norwich

What Makes Me Happy

Sports are the best
Holidays I can sit and rest
Weekends after the week of tests
See your family, that's the best
That's not all, there's more in store
Smile
Joy
Delight
Cheerfulness
Thrilled
Pleasure.

Money, money, money
Celebration time, come on!
Playing football on the telly
That's not all, there's more in store
Smile
Joy
Delight
Cheerfulness
Thrilled
Pleasure.

When are you happy?
I'm happy when I'm away from school
I'm happy on holiday
I'm happy on the PS4
I'm happy playing football.

Smile
Joy
Delight
Cheerfulness
Thrilled
Pleasure.

Happy.

Ben Johnson (10)
Hethersett VC Junior School, Norwich

POETRY EMOTIONS - Eastern England

School Disco Worries

School disco worries,
What to wear,
Oh my hair,
Life's not fair!
Oh will my friends be there?

Worry, worry, worry,
Worry in a flurry.

Can I dance?
Why not take a chance?
Will I get a glance?

Worry, worry, worry,
Worry in a flurry.

What about the embarrassment,
At the school gate,
That can't happen,
Not in front of my magnificent mate.

Worry, worry, worry,
Worry in a flurry.

I've danced all night,
I've had such fun,
Dancing with my friends
And everyone,
My legs are stiff,
My feet won't move,
I've had enough of being in the groove!

Worry, worry, worry,
Worry in a flurry.

And just when I think I'm worry free
The worry comes back to haunt me,
What about next time?

Ellen Whiting
Hethersett VC Junior School, Norwich

What Does 'Hope' Mean?

Hope can feel sad and happy too,
Hope can ask for different things,
But I'll just quickly explain to you.

Hope can mean . . .
A wish for yourself to have perfect health,
Shiny bling, zero stings and an expensive wedding ring,
I hope for cake,
A giant snake
And a brand new phone for goodness sake!

But hope can also mean . . .
A wish for others,
None for you,
That's pretty kind,
The best thing to do!

I hope you'll be . . .
As strong as your dad and as kind as your mum,
As smart as your sister and for hate, you'll have none!
If you wish for others,
You can write it in a card,
Hope you'll have a happy birthday,
Hope this Christmas was the best,
Hope you will get well soon,
You should really get some rest!

But hopes and dreams can shatter away,
You might not become king one day,
That's what you need to understand,
That life is not in Happyland,
In life you can't always say nope,
But one thing we can do is hope.

Abigail Astriani O'Dell (11)
Hethersett VC Junior School, Norwich

POETRY EMOTIONS - Eastern England

It's Just Life

Little sisters,
Big brothers,
What are you going to do?
Forks scratching on people's plates,
Before they start to chew.

Irritating,
Pests,
Pain in the neck,
Nuisances,
Hacking me off,
Getting on my nerves.

Mornings,
Bedtimes,
I don't want to sleep!
Really loud public talking,
Squeaking your shoe along the floor when you are walking.

Irritating,
Pests,
Pain in the neck,
Nuisances,
Hacking me off,
Getting on my nerves.

Loud sneezing,
Parents ignoring you,
Mum, Mum, hellooo!
Blocked-up ears,
Squeaky floorboards and chairs.
These are all the things that annoy me,
What annoys you?

Bea Boyce
Hethersett VC Junior School, Norwich

Fear Is Near

Fear, fear, it's always here,
You fear, I fear, we all fear something.
Rats, bats, gnats, cats,
There's fear deep inside.
Fear lurks in every deep, dark corner
And jumps right out at you.
So beware when you sleep
Because in the darkest of the night
Fear will jump into you.
Fear, fear, it's always here,
You fear, I fear, we all fear something.
Clowns, cattle, even a rattle,
There's fear deep inside.
Fear is always with you,
Fear is down the street,
Fear is at the zoo,
Fear is black and bleak.
Fear, fear, it's always here,
You fear, I fear, we all fear something.
Zombies, mummies, Dracula too,
There's always fear inside waiting for you,
Fear has a cloak
As dark as night,
So you can't see when he's coming
And he could be coming tonight.
Fear, fear, it's always here,
You fear, I fear, we all fear something.
Trains, brains, canes,
There's fear deep inside.

James Attfield
Hethersett VC Junior School, Norwich

Worry

Feeling shivery,
Curled up in a ball,
School,
Bullies
That's coming soon.

Thoughts that make you shiver,
Words you'll never forget,
Shadows watching your every step.

Getting lost at big events,
Medical injuries,
Bumping your head,
Every day nightmares appear,
You wake up and start to fear.

Thoughts that make you shiver,
Words you'll never forget,
Shadows watching your every step.

Being geeky,
Girls being cheeky
Behind your back,
Rumours going round,
I can't listen now,
It's going to be bad for me.

Thoughts that make you shiver,
Words you'll never forget,
Shadows watching your every step,
Shadows watching your every step.

Ruby Raynor
Hethersett VC Junior School, Norwich

Joy In The Mind

Joy is in the room,
It's my birthday soon.
Presents will be by the chimney,
Whoo.
I'm happy, bouncy, jolly,
It's bliss,
Skipping, jumping.
I just can't hold it in!
I'm waiting for a sleepless night,
Just can't wait to see the sight.
Glowing in the darkness by the fire,
I need the day to come,
It's my heart's desire.
I'm happy, bouncy, jolly,
It's pure pleasure,
Tomorrow,
Tomorrow,
Ahhh,
Tossing,
Turning,
In my bed,
Ouch,
I just banged my head,
Thoughts buzzing through my mind,
As I turn to the other side.
I'm happy, bouncy, jolly,
Today's the day,
Hooray.

Katie Banfield
Hethersett VC Junior School, Norwich

POETRY EMOTIONS - Eastern England

Anger

As he charged across the playground,
Everybody scattered,
The dreaded Anger was here
And he was ready to destroy.

His face was purple,
His fists were clenched,
He gritted his teeth,
His whole body tensed.

Stalking around the playground,
Glowering and hissing.
Rage had overpowered him,
It was as if his soul was missing.

Everyone was stuck in a nightmare,
Their blood was running cold,
They hated Anger with all their might
And wished that he would go.

Anger shrieked and cursed to the sky,
For he knew he was alone,
The cold hatred in people's eyes,
Eventually drove him home.

Everyone thanked their lucky stars,
Because the storm was over,
They could be happy again
Until next time . . .

Lilly Walker
Hethersett VC Junior School, Norwich

Fear

Trembling,
Stammering,
Weak at the knees,
Wide brown eyes.

Fear comes creeping,
White as a sheet.
You're feeling weak,
Sleepless nights,
Scared of heights
And there are always too many gruesome sights.

Trembling,
Stammering,
Weak at the knees,
Wide brown eyes.

Nervous and jumpy,
Throat all lumpy.
Spiders spooky,
Crawlies creepy,
You might feel like your heart is leaky.

Trembling,
Stammering,
Weak at the knees,
Wide brown eyes.

Fear can have you hypnotised.

Rebecca Smith
Hethersett VC Junior School, Norwich

Mixed Feelings

As Wrath cuddles up in my veins
I suddenly feel that I have no restrains.
Such feeling could occur to death
Which by critical definition means theft,
Breaking up hope and joy in its evil overcoming fumes of despair
And confusion.
I now realise that it was all an illusion,
So Rage and Jealousy have made no fusion
Like a great flooding fountain of understanding
Unlike a raging, erupting mountain.
I now look back and see that I was not very nice
Which may come at a great, great price
Like a heavy bowl of moulded rice.
I know now that I should have listened to everyone's advice,
I now feel enchanted,
Instead of how I would have mentally face-planted
As I now understand
I feel so very, very grand.
I am so excited
And am sure that everyone will be so awfully delighted.
I will no longer do fighting,
Now that I have eventually clear sighting
And this is my poem's ending,
Which I am now sending.

Lucas Scott
Hethersett VC Junior School, Norwich

Joyfulness

Feeling it bubbling up,
Up, up, up,
Like an emotional hot,
Jolly,
Smiley,
Leaping about!
Laughing,
Swirling,
Jumping all around!
Everyone you meet you greet,
Everyone you walk to you talk to,
Joy can come from all sorts of things,
Joy can come watching people sing,
Joy can come from having lots of bling,
Joy can come even if the day is boring,
Joy can come from absolutely nothing,
Jolly,
Smiley,
Leaping about!
Laughing,
Twirling,
Jumping all around!
Joyful,
That's how I love to feel.

Evie Sayer (11)
Hethersett VC Junior School, Norwich

POETRY EMOTIONS - Eastern England

Joy

On the finest tropical beach,
Where it is always sunny,
With delicious smells of fresh bleach,
Joy is one happy bunny,
The golden sand and crystal-blue sea
This is where Joy appears to me.

Kittens and puppies,
Chocolate and sweets
And lots of lovely fluffies,
When the newborn lamb first bleats,
On a sunny morning with piping hot tea,
This is why Joy appears to me.

Leaping like a bouncy ball,
Happiest colours, silkiest hair,
Name anything positive, Joy's always there,
Spreads the joy to you and all,
Jumping everywhere as high as a flea,
This is what Joy appears like to me.

Pain and death, over the years,
All over you, your dad spills his beer,
Loads of sorrow, everlasting tears,
This is when Joy disappears.

Lily Cook
Hethersett VC Junior School, Norwich

Anger Is Here

In a huff
Gone bananas.
You're the storm
That kills all flowers.
Siblings make you feel this way,
By punching, kicking right, OK.

Just like you're about to pop,
Scarlet like tomato hot.
Teachers, siblings,
Irritating, right?
But you can't do anything about your life.

Always told to stop and freeze
But she started it by calling me selfish,
A meanie
And an ugly girl.
It's unfair.
Why do I care?

Just like you're about to pop,
Scarlet like tomato hot.
Teachers, siblings,
Irritating, right?
But you can't do anything about your life.

Gracie Brand
Hethersett VC Junior School, Norwich

POETRY EMOTIONS - Eastern England

Sadness

Lives in the sky,
Feels left out,
Still gonna cry,
Without a doubt.

Face droopy,
Shoulders down,
Eyes watering,
With a frown.

Down in the dumps,
While making sad memories,
Sadness lurks
In her woolly jumper.

When you're sad
She will come,
Make you laugh
And have fun.

Grey, black, blue
Are the colours she likes too,
That's my poem,
What about you?

What does Sadness look like to you?

Charlie Kate Skinner (9)
Hethersett VC Junior School, Norwich

Hope

What can you see on a summer's day?
A beautiful butterfly, flying away.
Wishes a-growing,
Out of the ground,
A war is over,
Hope is found.

Friendship,
Warmth,
Tingling,
Peace,
Joy,
Colour,
Surprise,
Sensations.

Hope is a fairy waving her wand,
Hope is the sun, shining down bright,
Hope is fun,
Hope is magic,
Hope is you,
Our world.

Isabel Younger
Hethersett VC Junior School, Norwich

At The Beach

A happy day at the beach
Having lots of fun
I love collecting tiny pebbles
Playing in the sun
The sun is shining brightly
Ice cream melting very fast
Splashing in the sea
Having a blast!

Maisie Wells (8)
Hethersett VC Junior School, Norwich

POETRY EMOTIONS - Eastern England

Hope

I hope that I will be like them,
Scoring goals all day,
Living in a mansion
With really good pay,
Visiting new places,
Well wouldn't you like that?

I hope that I will be like them,
Sprinting as fast as a cheetah,
Swimming like a fish,
Climbing like a monkey,
Leaping as high as a kangaroo,
Well wouldn't you like to be like that?

I hope that I will be like them,
A great singer with loads of fans,
A famous actor in the best films,
An artist like Picasso,
An amazing author just like Jeff Kinney,
Well wouldn't you like to be like that?

Well wouldn't you like to be all of those?

Liam Stevens
Hethersett VC Junior School, Norwich

Happy Days

H appy days are the best
A nimations are really cool
P arties are really fun
P laying with Lego is epic
Y ears passed, they get better

D ifferent days are more exciting
A wesome birthdays just happened
Y ummy food so delightful to eat
S winging on the swing as high as I can go I'm full of joy.

Vaughan Walker (9)
Hethersett VC Junior School, Norwich

The Motivation Of Tornadoes

Do you know why tornadoes destroy our world?
Whilst we were building buildings they still only twirled.
It was down to a negative feeling you see,
The thing that kept them sane was jealousy.
Back in 92BC was when it began,
They sent in hurricanes to destroy the clan.
It was down to a negative feeling you see,
The thing that kept them sane was jealousy.
Vengeance was taken on the Roman Empire,
Killing people to the tallest of spires.
It was down to a negative feeling you see,
The thing that kept them sane was jealousy,
Revenge continued in the Viking times,
Sinking many ships of the finest pine.
It was down to a negative feeling you see,
The thing that kept them sane was jealousy.
It went on into the reign of King George,
When many were killed right up near a gorge.
It was down to a negative feeling you see,
What did and still does anger them is jealousy.

Oliver Battley
Hethersett VC Junior School, Norwich

Excited

Excited is a happy feeling,
It lives in the darkest places,
It comes out on your birthday and on Christmas Day,
It comes out when you're surprised,
Or when you're playing with your friends,
It jumps up and down,
Excited is as yellow as the sun,
Scales as shiny as the fish in the sea,
It wears a purple cape on his shoulders.

Zoe Rodgers (8)
Hethersett VC Junior School, Norwich

POETRY EMOTIONS - Eastern England

All About Joy

Joy has a glowing face and is always bright and colourful,
Over the moon with everything and will always give a cuddle.
You'll love Joy, she'll be your friend, she'll always cheer you up.
Joy wants an emoji dress and her hair always sticks up.
She leaps and dances at any time, everywhere she goes.
She'll try and be anyone's friend and always strikes a pose.
Joy is awesome and is always fun every single day.
You'll love her as soon as you see her and she'll be your babe,
Her cheeks are as red as roses,
She loves taking photos,
Her hair is as golden as the sun,
She is so much fun,
Joy is a delight
Because of her sight.
Joy is your best friend,
You'll be happy without end.
She's as light as a feather
And happy whatever the weather.
Joy is great,
You should be happy she's your mate.

Evie Wood
Hethersett VC Junior School, Norwich

Extreme Fear

Fear flows in shivers down your spine,
A feeling which is definitely not divine.
When you are scared it's a terrible time.
Terror is a blanket covering your eyes.
When you're in the dark, fright will rise.
Panic likes to twist your mind,
Like a burning devil that's very unkind.
Being tortured like a sorry soul in Hell,
Your mind is a damp, dark steel jail cell.

Jacob Want (10)
Hethersett VC Junior School, Norwich

Joy

Joy lives in the brightest of places,
Where the sunshine and bunnies play,
She is always there reminding you of the fun times that you share,
Full of hope that Sadness will never reappear.

Joy appears at the happiest of times,
A hug from a friend makes her all warm inside,
Fun days in the sun, happiest times of all,
A glowing feeling fills her mind.

Her face is like a pale rose,
Her blonde hair covers her face,
She's the happiest emotion around,
Everyone likes her, they always come to play.

The only way to make Joy go,
When Anger, Fear, Disgust and Sadness take control,
One push of a button and away she blows,
Twisting and turning, down she goes.
Anger and Sadness make her all sad inside,
But a smile makes her fill with joy once more.

Keira Hanrahan
Hethersett VC Junior School, Norwich

Jealousy

J ealousy is the green-eyed monster glaring at you with a stern look.
E ar-aching, repeatedly saying, 'It's yours, it's yours, it's yours.'
A nnoyingly, creating a shiver down your spine, racing against the time.
L oudly eating the inside.
O utspoken all my life.
U nderstanding life is hard, hopefully not behind bars.
S uddenly going up in flames, can't believe I lived.
Y ou go down Hickety Road, it may be a lie but that is life.

Luke Howland
Hethersett VC Junior School, Norwich

POETRY EMOTIONS - Eastern England

Joy

The sun is up,
I'm feeling joyful,
As I jump crazy around,
People looking joyful,
I'm graceful for the Earth,
I'm graceful because of the human population,
Nothing is better than being joyful,
Always be joyful for the world,
For God and for the human population,
Be happy like God,
Do not be angry,
So always have joy,
Never be scared,
God is looking after you,
So never be frightened
And always have joy,
Because joy means joyful
And joyful means being happy!
So always be joyful for joyful means happy!

Pedro Daniel Weresi (9)
Hethersett VC Junior School, Norwich

Joyfulness

J olly as an elf bouncing up and down on Christmas Eve
O ver the moon looking at the laughing baboon!
Y ay is what I say when I score a good goal
F riends and favourite programmes are what make me feel joy
U ncontainable joy as we get to the top of the roller coaster
L icking my lolly, while fussing my cute little puppy
N ed and Ted can come to my birthday party
E njoying my chocolate and sweets
S nuggling up with my teddy
S plashing in the pool on my summer holiday.

Henry Jack Bailie (10)
Hethersett VC Junior School, Norwich

Anger

Have you ever felt angry like me?
Go and sulk,
Or go explode like a grenade,
You might even end up in first aid!

Anger,
Mad,
Stressed and depressed!

If something gets cancelled,
Or has to be stopped,
Video gaming is my lot.

You might see the dark side of me,
If my brother turns off the TV.
Fighting, swearing, throwing your things,
Why do people keep annoying me?

Do you ever get angry like that?
Nobody has ever been angry like the Hulk of course,
But I am so sick of shouting until I am hoarse!

Cobie Mark Didwell (10)
Hethersett VC Junior School, Norwich

Happy

Happiness is beautiful.
My good friend is a star,
She is called Joy.
She makes my life happy.
Joy is bright yellow.
The best thing is she glows in the dark
Like normal stars.
When I'm sad she talks to me,
When it's tea Joy eats with me.
She is always there for me,
That's why I'm always happy.

Simone Awbery
Hethersett VC Junior School, Norwich

Happiness

Happiness is everywhere.
Happiness is within you.
Happiness is what you make it.
Happiness is true.

Happiness is birthdays.
Happiness is holidays.
Happiness is being fun.
Happiness is ecstasy.
Happiness is joy.
Oh boy.

Happiness is in my head like rush hour,
It is like a hot shower.

Happiness is being calm.
Happiness is everywhere.
Happiness is within you.
Happiness is what you make it.
Happiness is true.

Alex Amos
Hethersett VC Junior School, Norwich

Brave I Am

Bravely I clutch my sword with two hands,
While emerging from darkness,
Snarls become closer.
As a shiver trickles down my spine,
Like water running down a gutter.
Aggressively I lunge out into an open space,
Finally I managed to stab it in the belly,
Like a butcher chopping his meat.
Marvellously the dragon had been left defenceless
In a valiant manner
Without fear I managed to read lines out in assembly.

Ryan Walford
Hethersett VC Junior School, Norwich

Fear

Fear lives in the sneakiest of places,
Mostly under a garden bench,
Or in a little trench,
Never comes out of its shell.

Running around,
Being a clown,
These are things that make Fear appear
And you don't want to worry him!

He is orange,
With shattering teeth,
A crazy friend to meet,
Relaxing is a treat.

A deep breath
And a gentle blow,
Will release the flow,
Fear will be with you one day
So be sure to kick him away.

Alfie Baker
Hethersett VC Junior School, Norwich

Happy

Happy here is happy, as happy as ever,
As clappy as ever,
It's like opening a present,
He lives on a beach,
In a beach hut on the tide,
He's all bright and gold,
His feet are smelly,
He never cries,
He never hides,
He's always happy to come and play,
Call him and say, 'Yay!'

Toby Dunne (8)
Hethersett VC Junior School, Norwich

POETRY EMOTIONS - Eastern England

The Anger Inside

A deep, dark rage burning through,
Erupting inside it bursts out of you.
Frustration leads to this being shown,
The trigger remains forever unknown.

Anger lives in the most deepest of places,
Because of people pulling mean faces.
It builds up inside and bursts without warning,
Going all day, starting from the morning.

He's covered in red and full of might,
As strong as a bull starting a fight.
Fists clenched, my palms start to sweat,
Tears flooding my face, making my cheeks wet.

Take a deep breath and count to ten,
Returning the anger to its den.
They won't witness Anger for a while,
The last time I saw him, he was with a smile.

Leo Jones
Hethersett VC Junior School, Norwich

Anger

Anger lives in the deepest, darkest part of your nightmares
Where the monsters and demons are there, always ready,
To lash out at you and fiddle with your hair.
Always there if you say a word or if you hear a singing bird.
He is always there if you see him or not,
But be careful he might surprise you or not,
Wearing a suit with a black and white tie,
Getting red-hot like you're going to die,
The only way to stop him is to take a deep breath to gently blow him away.
Sunshine and cuddles and soothing words
Will make Anger disappear for days.

Olivia Partner (9)
Hethersett VC Junior School, Norwich

Anger Is Wild

Anger is wild, Anger is tough,
It hides in a temple where the night is rough.
Horrible creatures and everything mean
And eyes fierce green.

Anger is wild, Anger is tough,
In fact he is deep dark red,
Beware as you don't want to cross him
No running across him, people stay clear.

Anger is wild, Anger is tough,
In fact everyone hates him,
Playing games results in people being mean,
All he wants to do is scream.

Anger is wild, Anger is tough,
But he can disappear,
Try saying nice words or playing nice games
And he will soon be replaced with a smile.

Toby O'Dell (9)
Hethersett VC Junior School, Norwich

As I Lay Here

As I lay here
I'm shrouded in fear.
Watching the door
Forever more.
Trembling at every noise,
Cuddling my toys.
Very, very afraid,
Always scared of the blade.
Arachnophobia I have,
Feeling like a chav.
As I lay here
I'm shrouded in fear.

Luca Foster
Hethersett VC Junior School, Norwich

POETRY EMOTIONS - Eastern England

Anger

Anger lives in the darkest of places,
Where scary monsters hide.
Sadly sometimes it doesn't stay inside,
With a zip and bang he leaves my mind.

The rage of losing a game,
Or being called a nasty name.
It leads to me causing a mess,
And feeling a little stressed.

His face glows red,
Feeling stressed in his head.
Splinters sticking out of his thumb,
Nobody likes him, not even his mum.

The only way to stop him is to play,
Please don't run or hide away.
Sunshine and cuddles hide the rage,
Friends and family return it to its cage.

Harry Lacey (9)
Hethersett VC Junior School, Norwich

The Great Joy

Joy lives in your mind high in the sky,
Everywhere you go.
She can be in a cupboard or in a puddle,
She'll brighten your day if you're in a muddle.

She appears when you're happy,
She'll make your day fly by with fun,
Always enjoyed in the sun.

Joy is gold, bright and yellow,
Beaming and gleaming wherever she goes,
Her dress glowing like the sun,
She just makes everything fun.

Eleanor Ashling
Hethersett VC Junior School, Norwich

Sadness

Sadness lives up high in the sky
She's full of dullness you see
When she comes out she's a bag of tears
As a result of many fears.

She only appears when she's gone through heartbreak
She's full of dullness you see
She arrives all of a sudden
You'll find that you will soon be swimming in the sea.

Her face is chubby and completely blue
She's full of dullness you see
Her glasses sit on her cheeks gathering up more dust
When will her face stop looking so glum?

She disappears when something fun is happening
She's no longer full of dullness you see
A smile across her face
Makes the world a better place.

Elizabeth Barton
Hethersett VC Junior School, Norwich

Excited

Excited loves to come and play,
She loves to smile with friends,
Her joy lifts you up.
Excited has a wardrobe full of pink,
She wears colourful shoes,
Her clothing nearly blinds you.
She's a wonderful feeling in life,
Excited sings and dances around the floor.
She never needs help deciding what to wear.
Excited never frowns,
She smiles non-stop.

Marcia Holbrook
Hethersett VC Junior School, Norwich

POETRY EMOTIONS - Eastern England

Anger Poem

Anger is stuck in the darkest of places,
Living with days that are not wanted.
But sometimes he just can't control his temper
As he erupts, he can't stay inside.

Either being called names or people that are pains,
Simply being told off by grown-ups,
These are the things that make Anger appear,
And he's mean and he'll scream!

Anger is red and he has a big head,
That is full of frustration and hatred.
He wears dark clothes, that he never shows
Because no one likes what they see.

The only way to stop him, is to let the love shine through,
Or let Joy take over.
Make him hide away
So he won't ruin your day.

Ellis James Bane (10)
Hethersett VC Junior School, Norwich

The Day Of Excitement

Bursting with joy,
My birthday comes closer,
I jumped out my bed,
Feeling so hyper,
I rush down the stairs,
To see my family waiting there,
I open my presents,
To feel like the luckiest boy in the world,
Looking forward to my party,
As I wait for my friends,
I realise I have the best family in the world.

Kai Codie Clayton Gray-Williams (10)
Hethersett VC Junior School, Norwich

Joy

Joy lives in the highest of places,
Where the guardians and angels play.
When there's a problem,
She's ready to sort out the day.

Being ready to help when negativity appears
Or when a problem becomes clear.
Joy appears only with these
Ready to sort out the day.

Her face is golden, her skin smooth,
She's the best emotion around.
Everyone likes her, they all come and play,
She's ready to sort out the day.

She only retreats when a problem is solved,
Everyone content, playing again,
Sunshine, friends and sorry words,
Will make Joy happy once more.

Demi Wright
Hethersett VC Junior School, Norwich

In The Woods

As I entered the woods
It was cold so I put up my hood
I need more
So I explored
I heard a prowl
Maybe it was an owl
I'm not scared
I'm in a nightmare
I'm hungry, I need a pie
What emotion am I?

Tallulah May Blake (9)
Hethersett VC Junior School, Norwich

POETRY EMOTIONS - Eastern England

Anger Poem

Anger lives in the deepest forest,
Where the sun never shines,
No animals smile, they scatter in fear.
They haven't witnessed Anger for a while.

Being left out of games,
Getting hurt or bullied,
All make him appear.
They haven't witnessed Anger for a while.

His face red and bloodshot eyes,
Spikes appearing in a rage.
This creature inside has been released.
They haven't witnessed Anger for a while.

Sharing my problems,
And a pat on the back,
Finally it's listened to and causes a smile.
They won't witness Anger for a while.

Jamie Alexandra Reid (9)
Hethersett VC Junior School, Norwich

Happy

His heart is beating loud and fast,
He's full of happiness, he wants to have fun,
Making and baking, cooking cakes,
They had lots of spots and dots,
Laughing and full of happiness
He ate a cake that he baked,
Running in the sun when the snails are away
And while the clouds are awake,
Jumping and splashing in snail slime
Worms were digging in the mud.

Keira Stephens (8)
Hethersett VC Junior School, Norwich

Anger

Anger lives deep down
In the darkest caves,
At the bottom of the ocean,
How will I be saved?

Arguing friend over four square,
Or how a friends starts to star,
Anger appears at the darkest of times,
Nowhere to run, nowhere to hide.

A fountain of coloured, wild rapids,
Bubbling and popping,
Red, yellow and orange splatters,
Like a wild rabbit hopping.

The only way to stop him is to find a corner,
Take a deep breath, destroy,
Say something nice, try to be kind,
Soon you will find he quickly disappears.

Kyle Reeve
Hethersett VC Junior School, Norwich

Birthday Party

B ouncy castle,
I nvites handed out,
R ain, oh no,
T ry not to cry,
H appy,
D elicious ice cream and cake
A wesome birthday,
Y ellow presents.

Miya Porter (9)
Hethersett VC Junior School, Norwich

POETRY EMOTIONS - Eastern England

Joy

She lives in a cloud of dreams,
She lurks all around.
She'll help you eat through greens,
You'll get a pound for every smile.

Her favourite colours are yellow and blue,
She cheers you up if you are in a grump.
If you are good she will give you a wink,
If you are in a grump she will give you a hug.

She will give you hugs and kisses through the day,
She will comfort you,
She wanders to and fro,
She has a funky hairdo.

She likes you,
She loves you
And she'll cherish every moment of it,
Every day she'll make a new friend.

Lilia Violet Mercer (10)
Hethersett VC Junior School, Norwich

Happy Fears

Happy feels like scoring a goal.
Kicking the ball in the top of the corner.
Happy eats a big fat portion of chips.
He gets happy when he eats them.
Happy likes to open his presents.
Happy likes to pick flowers.
Happy loves to sleep.
Happy loves to win games.

Riley Copeland (8)
Hethersett VC Junior School, Norwich

Tears Can Be Happy

Sadness glows like a shining star,
She never harms anybody by far.
Big, blue, amazing eyes,
That could light up a million skies.

Beautiful, silky, purple hair,
Thoughts in my mind do not seem fair.
The negative, miserable, cold feeling inside,
It brings her down and makes her cry.

The horrible emotions getting to the brain,
Nothing can stop her from feeling very vain.
Shivering goosebumps lead to tears,
All of the emotions turn to fear.

Life can be tough when you're a bit low,
But nothing can stop her, it will always show.
Sadness will fade into the dark,
But she still has that wonderful spark.

Mia Evie Poll (10)
Hethersett VC Junior School, Norwich

Excitement For Winning My Eleventh Trophy

T urbo makes me go faster
R acing my favourite bike
O vertaking second place
P ower pulsing through my veins
H appiness winning my trophy
Y es, my eleventh trophy!

Leo Mallett (9)
Hethersett VC Junior School, Norwich

POETRY EMOTIONS - Eastern England

Life As Sadness

Everyone tries to cheer her up,
Everyone's hope is running out,
She's down in the dumps,
They're soon going to give up without a doubt.

Shoulders down,
Eyes watering too much,
She has a frown,
Still right down in the dumps.

She lives in the sky,
Up in the blue,
Always starting to cry,
Dries her eyes with tissues from the loo.

They cheer her up by counting to ten,
She dries her eyes and stops crying,
Can you remember that Christmas back when?
She will stop and go to the sky by flying.

Isabella Williams
Hethersett VC Junior School, Norwich

It's My Birthday

Excitement bubbles up inside me like a volcano ready to erupt,
I see presents piled up in my room,
I hear candles being lit.
I'm excited, just a bit.
My brain's bouncing up and down.
It's time to go downstairs.
It's time to have some fun.

Isabella Grace Brown (8)
Hethersett VC Junior School, Norwich

Sadness

Sadness lies in the deepest caves,
Struggling to escape the waves.
He sits on a rock, staring into space,
Trying to control this emotional race.

Sadness appears when all is dark,
A sad memory or you can't go to the park.
He strolls back and forth thinking hard,
But he can't escape the dark.

Sadness goes when love appears,
He simply fades away.
Happiness fills the air,
What a great day.

Sadness is grey all over,
He wears a brown winter jumper.
His eyes are black and his hair is white,
Trying to look good but he constantly fails.

Harry Garland Goddard (10)
Hethersett VC Junior School, Norwich

Untitled

Happy eats candy, he loves rolling in grass.
Happy likes rough rugby, he's squishy.
His favourite fruit is an orange.
If he sees an orange he takes it.
One day, one night he fell into a marshmallow river and chocolate.
He lives in the wonderful land with Hogwarts.
There the baddies are trying to find him.

George Simmonds (8)
Hethersett VC Junior School, Norwich

POETRY EMOTIONS - Eastern England

Joy

Joy lives in a beautiful beach hut,
Her dreams coming true,
As the family grew,
Bringing a smile to her face.

She appears in the summer
Making lots of memories,
Her generosity making others happy,
Bringing a smile to her face.

She wears a pair of rainbow heels,
Her heart pink dress floating, trying to impress,
Her yellow hair styled in a perfect plait,
Bringing a smile to her face.

Joy disappears as the winter arrives,
Feeling lost in a war, her smile hides.
As spring gets closer, she reappears,
Bringing a smile to her face.

Holly Rose Palin (10)
Hethersett VC Junior School, Norwich

Hatred

H ard to calm me down
A red menacing monster
T he angry machine
R epulsing
E veryone's anger is accelerating
D emolish Anger away.

Brogan Hood (8)
Hethersett VC Junior School, Norwich

Disgust

Green party clothes,
Flowing through the wind,
Letting the world see her beauty,
Never eating gross broccoli,
Saying no to people, oh that's disgusting.

Always very protective,
Finding ways to be the star,
Never letting people eat greens,
By the way she hates them.

Lashing her eyes,
To let the world know,
That she's back
In town.

She's always passionate,
Striking her pose,
Whilst everyone is looking out.

Grace Hawkins
Hethersett VC Junior School, Norwich

Shy And Worried

I'm really shy and I don't know why
I'm really worried 'cause I didn't eat my curry
I think I'm going to sleep
I need some marshmallow peeps
I'm singing really bad
I'm beginning to go mad.

Maryam Gillis (8)
Hethersett VC Junior School, Norwich

Poem Of Joy

Joy lives in the treetops and high up in the sky
On top of the hills is where she lies,
In a cottage surrounded by friends,
Hoping that her friendship never ends.

Seeing people happy, seeing people loved,
She appears on your doorstep waiting with glee,
Hoping that you're happy with what you can see,
Someone waiting for a big warm hug.

Her face is pink and bright,
Her skin as soft as a dog's fur.
A sparkle in her eye and a patch of glitter,
Makes everybody shine and shimmer.

Sadness and Anger make her disappear,
Tears falling and shaking with fear,
If you can't control you, you might lose sight,
Of the beautiful world that she makes pure and bright.

Dayna Kelly Arbon (9)
Hethersett VC Junior School, Norwich

Time To Go On Holiday

Jumping up and down
Waiting for that very day to go on holiday
Gliding through the air and waving down below
Bathing by the pool, watching people splash
Drinking lemonade and driving in the car
What a wonderful day to go on holiday.

Elizabeth Ottaway
Hethersett VC Junior School, Norwich

Sadness

Sadness lives in a lonely cave,
Where no one ever goes.
She sits on a rock thinking to herself
And rubbing her sore, sore nose.

She only appears in sad memories
Or even unhappy thoughts,
But if you look on the bad side of things,
You will always be distraught.

Her face the colour of pure blue
And cheeks rosy red,
Casual clothes covering her,
With sea-blue hair on top of her head.

The only way to stop Sadness,
Is to look at yourself and calm down.
Think happy thoughts of the future
And you will no longer have to frown.

Hannah Cox
Hethersett VC Junior School, Norwich

You'd Better Stay Away!

I go deep, deep down inside,
When I come out you'd better stay out,
I'm like a raging rhino,
I'll slash, I'll dash,
Stay back until I go back,
Into the darkest ash.

Alex Scott (8)
Hethersett VC Junior School, Norwich

POETRY EMOTIONS - Eastern England

Knock, Knock On The Door

Knock, knock on the door
I see something that looks very poor
It's standing there
Looks like it's in lots of despair
With a face that's about to scream
When you are in the losing team
I have felt this before
When your eyes are about to pour
When you're filled with so much sorrow
You wish it was tomorrow
Its face was all wet
Covered in sweat
Its mouth was as wide as a massive pie
Screaming with all its might
Its lungs became really tight
Its throat turned sore
And it sank down to the floor.

Thomas Small
Hethersett VC Junior School, Norwich

Happiness

Happiness is a beautiful feeling,
She always is laughing and smiling,
When needed for help she'll be around,
She is a bright yellow and has blue eyes,
When she comes to you
You will be happy.

Amelia Graver
Hethersett VC Junior School, Norwich

But What If . . .

It's like a ticking bomb inside me,
Ready to explode.
Excitement taking over,
But what if . . .
A countdown happens inside my brain,
As my heart thumps.
Shaking the ground like thunder,
But what if . . .
I'll be fine,
He'll laugh forever,
Never die,
But what if . . .
Anxiety comes for a visit.
The ground starts to shake,
Everyone turns
On that girl . . .
That girl will be me!

Maisie Beckett (11)
Hethersett VC Junior School, Norwich

Time To Play

Her head dripping with sweat
She just wants to come and play
She jumps out at teatime to talk about your day
She wants to jump out when something happy happens
Exciting is a brilliant feeling
What emotion am I?

Chloe Hayes (8)
Hethersett VC Junior School, Norwich

Depressed

Not a flower in the sun,
Feeling like a guy who's said a bad pun,
I've been laughed at
And been hated,
Feeling like a balloon that's been deflated.
Fading into darkness,
Never seeing light,
Feeling like a guy who's just lost a fight.
Always watching TV,
Never doing sport.
Feeling like I don't care if I get taught.
I can't do literacy,
Even if I have loads of time,
Feeling like I can't make any poem rhyme.
Never joyful,
None of this is a lie,
What emotion am I?

Ryan Turner
Hethersett VC Junior School, Norwich

Anger

Anger is everywhere,
My head is as hot as lava,
I feel like I can lift a house,
I feel like a hot cup of tea,
My head is so hot I need to do the ice bucket challenge,
I need to rest, my heart is nearly out of my chest!

Daniel Wengrow (8)
Hethersett VC Junior School, Norwich

Helpless

The guy who nobody helps for some odd reason.
The guy that lives in the darkest caves.
The caves are on the most lonely islands.

He only comes out when things are hard.
When things get hard he comes for bad measure.
When he comes you will feel small.

This guy makes you feel small.
Every time he comes your dread kicks in,
Nobody likes him and nobody helps him either.

To stop him stand up to your fears,
Never feel helpless.
Be brave,
Otherwise you will always feel him.

It's so good to have done good,
Nobody will disagree with that.

Jay Vanhinsbergh (9)
Hethersett VC Junior School, Norwich

Confused?

No beginning, no end
How, what, when?
It's like tangled string,
I'm so confuzeld!
Urgh!
I'm so confused I can't even say it right!
Uncontrollable,
It doesn't make sense!
My mind can't process it,
It's like a bewildered baffled dog.
I'm getting mixed up!
It's clouding my brain,
I'm so confused!

Toby Want (10)
Hethersett VC Junior School, Norwich

POETRY EMOTIONS - Eastern England

Anger Poem

Anger lives in the shadows and darkness,
His friends are nightmares and scary ideas.

He screams when forced to eat his greens,
Sometimes when he is told off he will appear.

He wears dark black and red clothes,
His fists are as hard as a table,
The emotion of smiling he doesn't like.

He goes away when the sun comes out,
He disappears with a smile, a laugh or happiness,
When Joy appears Anger always sneers off,
And he never listens to anyone.

Happy pictures always make him erupt
And he really enjoys destroying them,
But when it comes to scary and violent pictures
Anger loves to admire them.

Harrison James Corr (9)
Hethersett VC Junior School, Norwich

Hatred . . .

One day I found myself wearing an ugly shirt
So I just hid behind the tree of birch
But they soon found me and started to pound me
They laughed for ages
Then they thought my shirt was made from pages
Then I felt angry, then I felt hatred
So I punched them until they fainted
My face was bright red like a bull ready to charge
Soon they left me alone
And made my mam call me on the phone
Then later I felt normal
Better I was
And you could no longer see my sobs.

Kieran Poundall
Hethersett VC Junior School, Norwich

What Emotion Am I?

A trickle of sweat drips from my hands,
Thundering to the ground,
Waiting for the clock to scream,
Fear and excitement build up inside me,
Shaking with fear,
Bubbling with delight,
As the sun shines through the window,
Melting down on me,
Everyone is silent,
The teacher glares over at me,
Wondering if I will ever finish,
Never-ending feeling,
Finally the clock screams,
It's break time,
What emotion am I?

A: Nervous.

Amy Gorman
Hethersett VC Junior School, Norwich

The Anger Poem

Anger lives in the darkest of places,
Confusion surrounding the screaming sounds.
Is it the children or the hounds?

Clammy hands and a smiling face,
A feeling of hopelessness and sheer disgrace.
When friends are playing all day long,
You could even see his face grimacing
While smelling a pong.

If you see him, give him a grin,
Because you might even see him messing up the bin.
Don't get too near 'cause
He might send a spear.

Thomas Agnew
Hethersett VC Junior School, Norwich

Disgust

Disgust lives high in the sky,
Where there is nothing to defy.
Green trees fulfil the heavens
With bright juicy lemons.
When Disgust sees veg,
She gives us a right old wedge.

She appears from the back,
With a great big sack.
All vegetables, very tasty
But those mushrooms, please wasty!

Her hair is bright green like the leaves on a cabbage,
She can be easily seen as her face is so savage.

'No, no, leave me alone,
You mushrooms taste like stone!'
'These old stones are dusty, they taste yucky.'

Abigail Conway
Hethersett VC Junior School, Norwich

Disgust

That tiny little diva inside your head,
Criticising her friends
And laying on her bed,
How sad she can be without many friends
But she'll get over it with a little disgust in your head.

She lives in a palace all shiny and clean,
With incredible servants and amazing scenery,
When you come in,
She'll show off her stylish outfit,
Her awful personality gets her own way,
Just because everyone's afraid to say no,
She hates vegetables but it's the colour of her dress,
That's why she's got friends, it's because of her dress.

Chloe Youngs (9)
Hethersett VC Junior School, Norwich

Anger

Found in the depths of an uncontrollable volcano,
Monsters surrounding me, I shout, 'No!'
My arrival causes the happiness to stall,
But then I leave its wonderful ball.

I despise losing games
Or getting called names.
Why can't you let me in?
I'll take this anger and throw it in the bin.

My face all red,
Fire coming out of my head.
If you want to mess with me
You need to think again.

Flowers and butterflies
Make me want to hide
In the depths of my gloomy home.

Kassidy Howell
Hethersett VC Junior School, Norwich

Man Of Bravery

The strong, fearless man
Arose from the ground,
He had muscles of solid iron
And hair of brown silk,
But these dashing looks don't fool anyone,
For bravery is his strong point.

He performed stunts of madness,
Tricks of mayhem
And most of all never stood down,
He lifted a train,
With no pain
And he could do it again,
He even fought a lion pulling its mane.

Tom Barnard
Hethersett VC Junior School, Norwich

POETRY EMOTIONS - Eastern England

Anger Inside Your Head

Anger lives in the darkest of places,
Where volcanoes splutter,
Bursting like fire,
It cannot be contained.

Being left out of games
And being called names
Or eating up his peas,
These are the things that make Anger mad,
Forcing him to appear.

His face is all red from screaming too much,
He's the fiercest emotion around,
His arms are all spiky for poking emotions
And they're very round.

The way to stop him is to ignore him and let him float away,
Sunshine, cuddles and nice words will keep him away for days.

Sam Cozens
Hethersett VC Junior School, Norwich

Joy

Joy lives at the top of your body,
Where no monsters creep and everything's jolly,
A light glows, the wind blows,
Inside the brain where there's no pain.

His face is yellow,
He's a good fellow,
He never lets out a wail,
Merely shakes his tail.

With a smile Joy appears,
Beaming like a banana between your ears,
Something special makes him bounce
Like a lion ready to pounce.

Matthew Jacob Basham (10)
Hethersett VC Junior School, Norwich

Sadness

Sadness lives at the bottom of my soul,
It looks like a dark, cold, damp hole.
It crawls out like old warts.

Sadness appears when you're alone,
When friends turn away,
Names become stones,
And words become shouts.

Shades of blue, from dark to light,
Short or tall,
Loneliness and shy,
Sadness comes with great sight.

Open your eyes and look around,
Stars turn to dust,
A smile's upside down,
Dragging your heels, till you find your ground.

Milly Lightwing
Hethersett VC Junior School, Norwich

Joy

Joy is the best of happiness
Every day is special
Spending time with family
It's like petals on a flower.

When I'm full of happiness
I'm always thinking, hurrah!
When I see my happy bunny
I always see a star!

When I am super happy
I am always ready to smile
I sometimes get in a joyful flap
But every day is a magical time.

Melissa Battley (8)
Hethersett VC Junior School, Norwich

Anger

Anger is the deepest, darkest thing,
He lives underground,
Where there is no sound,
Near all of the monsters and demons.

He comes out his cave,
Shows his red steaming skin,
To everyone near the bin
And makes them run away.

Some people like him,
Some people hate him,
No one disobeys him,
Really everyone hates him.

People can stop him,
Slowly blow at him
And Anger will fade slowly away.

Dylan Nair (9)
Hethersett VC Junior School, Norwich

Joy

Joy lives in a candy town,
The happiest place to be.
Where rooftops are sugar cakes
And soda pop rivers like the sea.

Joy appears when people smile,
They laugh with a twinkle,
It can last a while,
When people are happy.

Her body is bright,
Yellow with a sparkly tint.
With her flawless blue eyes,
Shining in the light.

Gracie Lilian Chalcraft (10)
Hethersett VC Junior School, Norwich

The Tears Of Sadness

Sadness hides in a cave
Where all the flowers droop
Life is very unfair,
Somewhere down there.
Being left alone or missing out
Losing or being called names
Life is very unfair,
Somewhere down there.
A pale bluey-green figure
Whose cheeks are red with tears.
Life is very unfair,
Somewhere down there.
Cuddles and sunshine,
Family and friends,
Life is comforting with them,
Somewhere down there.

Harriet Lewis
Hethersett VC Junior School, Norwich

Continue

Continue the words I write on the page,
These hands are frail, I have begun to age.
My arms are weak, I trail my feet,
These thoughts shall always be new.

Continue the words I write on the book,
This head is ancient and always shook.
Live forever, decrease never,
This thought shall always be new.

Complete the words I write in this piece,
These hairs have thinned, it's time to release.
Born loving, death to coffin,
I shall always be new.

Nia Peres
Hethersett VC Junior School, Norwich

Sadness

Sadness is the opposite,
To what everyone likes.
It's dark and gloomy,
Without any light,
Like a demon losing the will to live,
I stand there,
Waiting to whine because of my limbs,
I went to hospital with tears,
Trickling down my ears,
When I arrived I went to sleep,
Without counting any sheep,
As I woke up I jumped with joy,
But suddenly hit my toe
And I fell down and cracked my head,
I was there,
Lying . . . dead.

Lewis Duale (10)
Hethersett VC Junior School, Norwich

Happy Poem

H igh, high, high in the sky, someone else is flying by
A s she jumps high today she is not going to stay
P atting your friend very kindly
P laying happily with your friend
Y es this will never be the end.

Sara Barulho Rebocho Verweij (8)
Hethersett VC Junior School, Norwich

The Big Bad Monster

Over time he built up inside
Nowhere to run, nowhere to hide
Someone bellows or is just being mean
Erupting at last, he just wants to scream!
Losing games and being called names
It is no one's gain to be so insane
For the big bad monster has come again
To explode into red-hot flames
And cause a lot of pain.
A deep dark red bursting through you
Horns so rough it will toughen you up
Confusion leads to this being shown
The big bad monster is no one's fool.
From a glimpse of a friend,
It makes anger grow
It has realised it has no place inside.

Toby Cawdron (9)
Hethersett VC Junior School, Norwich

Excitement

Lighting up the world around me
Getting ready for the day ahead
It's going to be so much fun
I can't wait
The time is nearly here.

Grace Cole (9)
Hethersett VC Junior School, Norwich

POETRY EMOTIONS - Eastern England

Fear May Visit You One Day

Fear may visit you one day,
But he is actually OK.
You may see his
Large eyes under a bench,
Or maybe in a little trench.

Fear may visit you one day,
But he is actually OK.
You may see him,
Wrapping himself in bubblewrap,
Or maybe he is doing some tap.

Fear may visit you one day,
But he is actually OK.
You may
Give a gentle blow
But he will jump and go.

Rebecca Birchall (10)
Hethersett VC Junior School, Norwich

Joy

Floating high through a sky of blue
When you're in need of a friend, she's there for you.
Happily sitting by your side at night
Ready to remove every fright.

She appears with a smile
From ear to ear.
Glowing from head to toe
With a long flowing dress and a little blue bow.

A heart-warming face
Greeting passers-by
Day in, day out,
She's there for you,
Ready to lend a helping hand.

Elizabeth Sharpe
Hethersett VC Junior School, Norwich

Disgust

That tiny little diva crawling inside your head,
Just wants disgust
And mayhem too,
She doesn't do much, just to have disgust.
She also criticises her fellow friends,
She wants fame,
But she normally doesn't get it.

When she wants stuff give it to her,
Otherwise she'll get annoyed
And won't be your friend,
Even though she is quite a bossy girl,
She also has a very sweet heart.

She always has the latest fashion,
So watch out, she brags all the time
And don't forget stay away from her little mouth.

Jasmine Swenson (9)
Hethersett VC Junior School, Norwich

Anger

A nger is a hard feeling,
N ice is the opposite of Anger,
G rowling like a bear every day,
E motions of Anger are really frustrating,
R ed faces like angry snakes.

Hannah Ayu O'Dell (8)
Hethersett VC Junior School, Norwich

POETRY EMOTIONS - Eastern England

Rough

Rough is a minion of Anger,
Always fighting, always sad.
Grizzly deep voice, gravelly mad.
Muscly and broad, he can't ask for more,
He'll kick, he'll punch and never lets go of his past.

He lives in the deep of the world, lonely, sad,
But sometimes he breaks out all mad,
Hitting anything in his path.
But all he finds is he's mad, sad, lonely and moaning.
Don't be sad, all it does is make him mad.

You can be kind and not afraid of him and maybe he'll go back.
See, don't be sad and mad, be kind not bad.
His face pale and damp scares all around.
Deep leather suit, mysterious mask, skinny black shoes,
Big leather hat, crazy red eyes, scar stretching down an eye.

Joseph Mares
Hethersett VC Junior School, Norwich

Happy

H appy birthday
A lways excited
P eeping quietly
P eering through
Y ou can be happy too.

Layla Mai Watts (8)
Hethersett VC Junior School, Norwich

Sadness

Funny thing Sadness,
As black as black.
Never seen for long,
The chubbiest thing you know!

He lives deep down,
Out of human reach,
Making everyone cry,
But also very shy,
The mysterious figure remains hidden,
Until someone sheds a tear!

To keep Sadness at bay,
You must do this exercise every day,
Trust me it'll really pay,
So go outside every day,
To make Sadness go away.

Tom Tooley
Hethersett VC Junior School, Norwich

Party

P opping presents open
A t the party we play fun games
R unning around. Are you worn out?
T alking to my best friends
Y ou and me, having fun.

Harry Cheal (8)
Hethersett VC Junior School, Norwich

POETRY EMOTIONS - Eastern England

The Harmful Mind

Hate can decide
A friendship's fate.
Hate can proceed and progress
Through your kind
Until it finds
The harmful mind.
The bully
The one who loathes
The ones who wear clean clothes.

You pass Hate around as well,
We're all humans and we can tell,
But you can deflate Hate so it doesn't stay like Hell
But if you don't
You may as well stay in your house
Still hating a mouse.

Adam Abu-Elmagd (10)
Hethersett VC Junior School, Norwich

Is The World Really That Amazing?

Broccoli, eurgh! Carrots, eurgh! All these things I hate!
It's not up for debate!
Poets make the world sound lovely,
Lots of sunshine and flowers!
But they don't talk about:
The slime and sludge
And ugly pugs,
It makes my stomach tug!
Even our teeth black and grimy!
An' great big blisters and pus!

So God, is our world as majestic
As poets make out?

Oliver Watson
Hethersett VC Junior School, Norwich

Humble Poem, Not

Mr Humble thinks he's great,
He goes on and on about it.
'Oh, I've got the best shoes.'
'Oh, I have more money than you.'

When he walks past homeless people in the street
He will walk away and think to himself,
Look how terrible they look, I am glad to be the best,
He will stick his nose in the air, to all the people over there.

On Christmas Day when the Queen does her speech,
Mr Humble will stick his head in the air,
Showing off his greasy hair.

Mr Humble doesn't have any friends, no, not one,
People hate him for what he does.
They will never forgive him for what he's done.

Keela Ailis Olive
Hethersett VC Junior School, Norwich

Hatred

Hatred is a thing that lies in the darkest places,
He always has the droopy faces.

He wears the dullest clothes,
Where he lives no joy flows.

His voice is deeper than a blue whale
And when he's angry he chucks hail.

No one likes him, he has no friends,
Hatred is a feeling that never ends.

The only way to make him go away
Is to take a deep breath and blow him to the motorway.

So you're lucky, you've never come across Hatred
But when you do he'll make you go boohoo.

Jack Barnard
Hethersett VC Junior School, Norwich

Delighted

She lives in a castle,
Under the sea,
Away with the mermaids,
Swimming as happy as could be,
When you're sad,
She plays with your mouth,
She makes you smile for over a mile,
She comes at Christmas,
Don't forget birthdays,
She waits all year,
Just so she can appear,
Yellow, green, blue, they're her favourite colours too,
She makes you hyper when it matters,
The game she plays,
They always include you!

Lucy Ann Bradford (9)
Hethersett VC Junior School, Norwich

Happy

Hooray, it's the day,
My birthday of course,
I have bubbles in my throat
And a tingle of glee.
Happy is a wonderful feeling,
She makes my body feel great at any time,
She'll never shy away from a slice of fun.
Everyone loves her including me,
She never lets me down
And she always has my back.
I never want her to leave.
She wears a light blue dress,
With short blue hair.
I'm happier than ever with her next to me.

Madeleine Houlihan (9)
Hethersett VC Junior School, Norwich

Anxiety

The walls pushing in on me,
Like I'm being eaten up by my worries.
People laughing at me,
Judging me,
Like I have no feelings.
Deep down in a sea of darkness,
I can't take it anymore.
The world has turned upside down,
Like a never-ending nightmare.
People trying to break me.
I'm no glass sculpture.
I do have feelings
And nobody can take them.
I can be brave,
I've just never tried.

Maria Kenny
Hethersett VC Junior School, Norwich

Wandering Alone

The moon was the brightest spotlight,
Above the meandering river.
The wind blew quickly but silently,
Upon the high willow trees,
Wind shattered the dark moulded leaves.
I strolled through the gloomy forest,
Until I came to an abandoned field.
Suddenly I saw a dark shadow,
At first I thought it was a statue,
Then I wasn't so sure.
The shadow got closer and closer,
So with great fear I ran,
Glaring behind me, too busy to see,
That something else was following me . . .

Joshua Wright
Hethersett VC Junior School, Norwich

POETRY EMOTIONS - Eastern England

Fear

Spiders crawling all around your home,
If you don't squash them more will start to roam,
Wriggling in the basement deprived of light,
If you see one it will give you a fright.

In your sleep you see strange shapes,
When you come closer they look like white capes,
One turns around and so do the rest,
Then they shriek at you, 'That food looks the best!'

When you go right through a door,
Your brother jumps out and does a roar,
You almost faint,
You almost fall,
He uses you as bait,
Then shoves you on the floor.

Oskar Krolak
Hethersett VC Junior School, Norwich

Joy

Joy plays with boys,
Who play with their toys.
He's yellow, blue, red,
He's multicoloured.
Oh this is fantastic,
He's more Joy than I've seen him.
He's truly Joy,
He cheers people up.
He's really nice
Until mice come.
He's really popular,
You will never forget him.
He is honest!
So that's Joy!

Ioan Warren
Hethersett VC Junior School, Norwich

Disgusted Feeling

Disgust gives me a shiver in my bones,
She always hates to eat her greens,
She'll push away her broccoli, sprouts and peas,
Disgust is always popping from under your ribs.
She's all light green with vomit on her scarf,
Disgust is a gross feeling,
You won't want it too often,
You'll fail to get her to eat her tea
And to stop throwing food at you,
Disgust has green greasy hair,
She'll never stop picking her nose
And eating the contents,
Although Disgust saves me sometimes,
She won't take being told no!

Gemma Walford
Hethersett VC Junior School, Norwich

Anger

A really annoying house
N aughty Anger feels bad
G roups all around growl
E ffects can change your life
R estless that's what I feel.

Isaac Lawson Ford (9)
Hethersett VC Junior School, Norwich

Anger

Anger is a horrible feeling
It's the worst feeling in the world
It lives in the deepest, darkest places
It eats all of the other feelings
So you need to stay away.

Johnny Henri (8)
Hethersett VC Junior School, Norwich

Happy

Happy lives in the lightest places that can be,
It's like a little monster that lasts forever,
It loves to eat colourful fluttering flowers that make it get stronger,
Happy is like a furry friend.
When you feel sad Happy comes and makes you feel happy.

Lucy Tull (8)
Hethersett VC Junior School, Norwich

Anger

A nger is a fierce creature.
N o one can escape when he's awake.
G oing around scaring everyone.
E veryone will scream.
R unning and shouting when Anger is awake.

Gabriel Escalera
Hethersett VC Junior School, Norwich

POETRY EMOTIONS - Eastern England

Love

L ife is the best
O rder a beautiful box of chocolates
V acation is on hold
E verything is amazing.

Erin Barrett (8)
Hethersett VC Junior School, Norwich

Joy

Joy is yellow, like a stupendous spring
Joy is beautiful like a shiny diamond ring
Joy is delicious like sweet caramel ice cream
Joy makes me want to have a crazy daydream
Joy smells amazing like gorgeous white roses
Joy makes me feel the pop music
In my dance I should use it
Joy looks like young children having lots of fun
Now I see the bright shining sun
Joy sounds like somebody's sarcastic laugh
Let's go to the cool swimming bath
Joy feels like a bed that's soft and smooth
I never want to move
Joy.

Nyesha Moran
Radford Primary School, Nottingham

Anger

Anger is red and dark lava, it spat orange
Very hot, hotter than porridge.
It tastes like magma rocks and ash from an erupted volcano.
It is louder than a rhino
And smells like burnt obsidian and giant fire stones.
It yells loudly and moans.
It looks like painted volcanoes thrown on fire boulders.
It is just furious like deadly withered daredevils
And a monstrous beast.
The use of badness will never cease.
Anger feels like an eroded zombie
And a mutant monster
Now I will make it tougher.

Zain Afzal (9)
Radford Primary School, Nottingham

Disgust

Disgust is a lighter green with long eyelashes
She tastes like mouldy black broccoli on a Sunday pizza
And out-of-date gravy and Brussels sprouts
Disgust smells like vanilla perfume and ice-snow all over
She looks like broccoli wearing a pink scarf with polka dots
With a green and purple dress with green shorts
Disgust sounds like a bird in the sky but she talks a lot
She feels fuzzy and feels like baby skin
Although she loves to win
She ran around like mad and started to spin
She has a weird-shaped chin
Although she has a cheeky grin.

Ellie Butler
Radford Primary School, Nottingham

POETRY EMOTIONS - Eastern England

Joy

Joy is pink like a rose
On top of a bush
It tastes delicious like sweet
Strawberry cake
Joy looks like a small sweet
Teddy bear and sounds
Like kids
Laughing in the park
It feels like the sun rising again
Yes, we are forever friends, I hope this
Day never ends.

Tayezja Engelmann
Radford Primary School, Nottingham

Anger

Anger is red like a flaming fire
It tastes like mouldy hot volcanoes
It is as furious as a lion
It is as angry as a stampede
Anger smells like a smoke steaming fire
It looks like a horrifying person
Sometimes like a demon
Sometimes his heart kills
Anger sounds like a bull, an eagle, and a monster
It feels like a demon and an evil witch's rotten hands.

Jamarne Ramone Richards (10)
Radford Primary School, Nottingham

Anger

Anger is like people making me feel angry
Its tastes like rotten zombies
Anger tastes like revolting rotten flesh
It looks like your heart is beating, breaking
Anger sounds like a horrible, bad devil
Anger feels as furious as a tiger
Anger is as hot as a sun but is not really fun
Anger smells like a pot of hot lava.

Zain Ali
Radford Primary School, Nottingham

Anger

Anger is blood-red with a fiery kick
It tastes like lava from a volcano and the Earth's core
It smells like a million hot peppers with nuclear nitrogen dioxide
It looks like a red and fiery demon devil
And sounds like the screeching of a thousand cackling witches
Anger feels like a spiky plant piercing your skin
Like a blackout again and again
Going through an endless chain of pain.

Trey Luke Barrett-Griffiths
Radford Primary School, Nottingham

POETRY EMOTIONS - Eastern England

Fear

Fear is bold and black like an empty room
It tastes like revolting socks
And smells like stinky skunks
Fear is the sight of one lonely person
It sounds completely silent
Fear feels like a snake on your neck
It feels like a nervous wreck.

Ayaan Khan
Radford Primary School, Nottingham

Anger

Anger red and hot as lava
It tastes like burnt orange in the sun
And smells like an old volcano
Anger looks like flames coming out of your mouth
It sounds like wind whooshing away
And feels like a bad migraine
Now I feel the pain.

Humayd Muhammad
Radford Primary School, Nottingham

Anger

Anger is as red as dried blood
It tastes like burnt toast and mud
And smells like furious, fiery smoke
Anger looks like a dim-lit, dark room
It sounds like a wicked witch cackling on a broom
Anger feels like a thump in the face
And feels like a big disgrace.

Sara Benarab
Radford Primary School, Nottingham

Disgust

Disgust is green like eating rotten green tomatoes
It tastes like chocolate with cauliflower

Disgust looks like slimy sick all over the floor
And smells like a whole house stinking from revolting broccoli

It sounds like someone belching all day
Disgust feels like swimming in vomit some way.

Aaqib Basit Muhammad (10)
Radford Primary School, Nottingham

POETRY EMOTIONS - Eastern England

Heartbreak

Heartbreak is as black as the Devil
It tastes like poison ivy
Heartbreak smells like rotten eggs
Heartbreak looks like Hell
It sounds like all the darkness in the world emerging
Heartbreak feels like someone has taken your true love.

Joshua Dzima
Radford Primary School, Nottingham

Fear

Fear is blue and cold like a mountain with spooky, slimy mud
It tastes like milk with blood
And smells like smoke and rotten eggs
Fear looks like a dead family
It sounds like someone talking to a bloody girl with dark hair
Fear feels like spiders walking on your body.

Emilia Diduch
Radford Primary School, Nottingham

Anger

Anger is red, fiery hot
It tastes like blood and flaming peppers
Anger smells like a smoky sky
It looks like a booming bomb waiting to explode from a ragged dome
It sounds like a T-rex roar, louder than a Minotaur
Anger feels like a Minotaur, stronger than an asteroid.

Shemaraye Colbourne-Smith (10)
Radford Primary School, Nottingham

Disgust

Disgust is green like mouldy broccoli
It tastes like expired cabbage with gravy
And smells like Cheddar cheese on Brussels sprouts
It sounds like slimy sick oozing out of someone's mouth
Disgust feels like silky soft cauliflower crumbling in your hand
Sometimes it feels like firm sand.

Ami Zogaj (10)
Radford Primary School, Nottingham

Heartbreak

Heartbreak is red like a red firefighter,
Heartbreak tastes bitter,
It smells like old smelly socks,
An eagle crowing,
Heartbreak feels like someone punching me with a hard fist,
It's like being attacked by a bull.

Kasra Khalilipir
Radford Primary School, Nottingham

Anger

Anger is burning red and flaming hot
It tastes like a hundred hot peppers in your mouth at once
Anger smells like a barbecue gone wrong
It looks like a burning bonfire
Anger sounds like a devil killing your friend.

Taryn Blackband
Radford Primary School, Nottingham

Lost

When you feel lost, you're scared and lonely,
For a while you wait and wait, thinking they'll come back.
You realise they won't, and run back and forth,
Thinking of a plan and also remorse
Yes, you got it I can now go home
But wait, you forget and run out of glee.
Your lip starts to tremble, and your tears stream
I'm never getting back, I'm gonna die here
It's a fight of sadness and instinct
Will they forget me, or cry every day?
I bite into my lip and stare at one spot
People around me, ignore me and look away
Finally yes, someone notices me
He asks where I live but I say where I'm meant to be
He lives in the area I say, so he's confused
He brings me in his house with his daughter and wife.
When I come in he finally calls the police,
Soon I can finally go back home
First sight of my parents I feel happy and safe again
Being lost is more terrible than you think
People get lost in all sorts of places
Like woods, forests, also foreign countries
So if you go somewhere different, know your surroundings
And then you won't feel the experience I felt.

Tyler Gordon (11)
St Michael's VA Junior School, Norwich

POETRY EMOTIONS - Eastern England

Worries

You ever get that feeling?
The butterflies in your tummy
Yeah, there's no healing,
When you just want to eat something scrumny.

Well I sure have,
Sometimes it's good,
Sometimes it's bad.
I wish I could
Get rid of this feeling
With no healing.

I've missed the deadline
All this worry is for my mum and dad.
It's sending chills to my spine
This is all quite bad.
Can't get rid of this feeling
With no healing.

They're getting a divorce,
I wish they weren't
Well I can't stop them of course
My life and soul are burnt
That's the feeling
With no healing.

It's all my fault,
They're not together
It's clearly not together forever,
Shouldn't have been born
Life has been torn
This is the feeling
With no healing.

Candece Kerslake (11)
St Michael's VA Junior School, Norwich

The Night

Blurry blackness covering the sky,
Seeing the stars shimmering in the night,
The night, the night,
Surrounding the sky,
The moon is glistening like a comet
Soaring brightly in the night sky,
Wondering, dreaming,
The night, the night,
It overwhelms me,
I gaze with wonder,
No one knows what's out there,
It could be anything,
I just wonder and wonder,
The night, the night,
It feels so wondrous yet so depressing,
The night, the night,
Sometimes night isn't all that bad,
Just imagine
Someone in your family who has passed away
Is in the stars,
Gazing at you,
They see you every night,
The night, the night,
They still love you no matter what,
You're precious to them,
You will never leave their hearts,
Remember that, remember,
They love you
It's the night.

Natalia Witucka (11)
St Michael's VA Junior School, Norwich

POETRY EMOTIONS - Eastern England

Fear

When your hands twist and turn,
When you just want to run into her arms,
When you can't learn,
Fear, that's what it's called.

Fear, fright,
There's loads more I could write,
Butterflies so spinning round and round,
Like a nightmare at night,
Fear, is what it's called.

You feel like it's never-ending,
Like you're on a deserted island with no way back,
It feels like the joy in my soul is descending,
It's like there's no going back,
But one day it will change,
I know it,
I'm just waiting,
And I always will,
Fear, is what it's called.

Teagan Berry (11)
St Michael's VA Junior School, Norwich

Sombreness

Conversation is a lock of time,
Calm but still a matter of depression,
An unnatural state of stillness,
Joy is sucked out of your heart,
Grave glance or stare,
Thoughtful of your every move,
Reacting to others is never the case,
An army of drab, colourless clothing,
Gazing away to avoid eye contact,
Sombreness.

Alexis Venzon (11)
St Michael's VA Junior School, Norwich

Anger

Anger is when you clench your fists,
Anger is a feeling you can never ignore,
Anger is a raging fire,
Anger will dig right down to your core,
Anger you shoulder, never admire.

Anger is a stormy day,
Anger could come any time,
Anger never likes to play,
Anger is never fine,
Anger is something you can never control.

Anger could hurt someone's feelings,
Believe me Anger is a horrible nightmare.

Isla Sistern (11)
St Michael's VA Junior School, Norwich

Anger

I am Anger,
I always feel angry
Whenever I'm angry my head bursts out with lava,
I never join in with laughter,
When I'm angry I'm always rough,
Punching, kicking, throwing things.
I try to stop myself
But I can't,
I'm Anger,
And Anger is me,
I dig my nails right into my skin
That's how I live my life.

Lillia Bettcher (11)
St Michael's VA Junior School, Norwich

POETRY EMOTIONS - Eastern England

A Riddle

Volcano in my tummy,
It's going to erupt,
Some mean words are coming out,
People are horrified without a doubt.

I'm just about to explode,
I have gone into bad mode.

I'm furious, fierce, I'll give you a fright,
When people look it's not delightful,
He is looking for people to be spiteful.

He is as bad as a demon.
What emotion am I?

A: Anger.

Leo Cridland
St Sebastian's CE Primary School, Grantham

What Emotion Am I?

I can't wait to get home,
I don't like domes,
I'm not angry at all
And I do like balls,
I'm as leapy as a frog,
I love dogs,
I go down low,
I can tie a bow,
I feel so tingly tangly,
Like I have fairy dust in my tummy,
I like my mummy.

What emotion am I?
A: Happy.

Fenton Gregorich (8)
St Sebastian's CE Primary School, Grantham

What Emotion Am I?

What emotion am I?
I am as joyful as ever
And I care for others.
I am delighted to the brim
And when my pod opens I feel very jumpy.
And as the day ends I feel as cold as ice.
I feel so jolly every day
And when I feel sad I turn away and say
I will always have friends.
I'm always overjoyed in every way all day.
I am excited, my colours are red, pink, blue and yellow.
My heart huddles and hurls around,
Light like a feather.

Phoebe Turner
St Sebastian's CE Primary School, Grantham

What Emotion Am I?

Feeling worried about something new
I'm too scared to say peekaboo.

Wherever I go is a stranger
And when I go it's disturbing danger.

I feel really grey
I never know what to say.

When someone says, 'Boo!'
I go, 'Cuckoo!'

I feel like I'm going to cry.
What emotion am I?

Georgi-Lea Askew (9)
St Sebastian's CE Primary School, Grantham

POETRY EMOTIONS - Eastern England

What Emotion Am I?

It's like dynamite in my belly,
I'm scared I might hurt someone
But I don't want to,
I'm scared that I might give someone a fright,
My heart is thumping,
I'm as red as the sun,
It feels like a volcano about to explode,
I think I'm going to hurt someone
And hopefully no one can stop me.

What emotion am I?
A: Anger.

Bobby Gregorich
St Sebastian's CE Primary School, Grantham

Excited

My heart is with laughter,
My arms are joyful,
My fingers are sizzling,
My legs are shaking,
My toes glitter with a smile,
My eyes are shiny,
My lungs are smiling with excitement,
My brain gives me lots of energy,
My stomach goes lighter and lighter.

What emotion am I?
A: Excited.

Tom Manning
St Sebastian's CE Primary School, Grantham

My Emotion

A fire burns inside my tummy,
You just want to run to Mummy,
It's like being on a lead,
You feel as small as a bead,
I want to scream,
But my tongue won't work,
Suddenly the air gave a great big jerk,
Then I was as free as a bee.

What am I?
A: Fear.

Darwyn Temple (8)
St Sebastian's CE Primary School, Grantham

What Emotion Am I?

I am like a red bull
My heart is pumping like crazy
My face is red
My hand is like steel
Ready to punch someone
As spiky as needles
I will hurt you
I will not be there for you.

What emotion am I?
A: Angry.

Marcis Lilientals
St Sebastian's CE Primary School, Grantham

POETRY EMOTIONS - Eastern England

What Am I?

Lovely singing in my head.
Flowers growing in my bed.
Sunny days every day.
School is fun, we are brave.
Friends are together, my heart is made.
Lovely love for other people, I am feeling yellow.
Lovely light!

What am I?
A: Happiness.

Poppy Harding (8)
St Sebastian's CE Primary School, Grantham

Emotion Riddle

I feel like I'm going to burst with rage.
I'm going to rage and pump until I calm down.

My hand feels mean,
Ready to punch!

If I talk about it,
My feelings go away.

What emotion am I?
A: Anger.

Lily Chivers (8)
St Sebastian's CE Primary School, Grantham

A True Emotion

I'm very, very gloomy
I'm very, very glum.

I'm really, really not in the mood
I think I've gone numb!

My mum says I've just got out of the wrong side of bed
My dad says I've got a tired head.

I'm very, very droopy today
I think I'll just go to bed!

Hattie Raeburn (8)
St Sebastian's CE Primary School, Grantham

Riddle

I feel like a volcano
Ready to erupt
My heart feels like a tornado
Spinning on its own
My hands are ready to battle
Look out, I'm dangerous!

What emotion am I?
A: Anger.

Leo Kavanagh
St Sebastian's CE Primary School, Grantham

Riddle

My first is in super and also in jumpy
My second is in giggling but not in mumbling
My third is in light-hearted but not in calm
My fourth is in laughing but not in whimpering
My fifth is in happy but not in angry

The monster tickles me and I feel this emotion.
What emotion am I?
A: Silly.

Vinnie McGregor Price (8)
St Sebastian's CE Primary School, Grantham

What Emotion Am I?

I'm full of hugs and kisses,
My hands are really grippy,
You'd better dash
Because he will squeeze you to death.
Like a kissing machine
Or a hugging machine.

What emotion am I?
A: Love.

Warren James Jackson (8)
St Sebastian's CE Primary School, Grantham

What Emotion Am I?

I felt like I was going to explode
A volcano erupting in my stomach
Colours began to flash in my head
Oranges, yellows, greens and red
I felt like a lightning bolt about to strike
And a tornado trashing everything in sight.

What emotion am I?

James Martin (8)
St Sebastian's CE Primary School, Grantham

What Emotion Am I?

I have a bull in my heart.
People are scared of me.
My fist is getting ready to punch.
I hate people when they annoy me.
I am so emotional.

What emotion am I?
A: Angry.

George Crompton-Allan (8)
St Sebastian's CE Primary School, Grantham

POETRY EMOTIONS - Eastern England

What Am I?

Rampaging, it's horrible, I cannot hold it in.
I'm ever so scared, I might hurt someone.
I'm turning red, what shall I do?
In a second I'm going to shout . . .
'Argh!'

What emotion am I?
A: Anger.

Lucy Hewitt
St Sebastian's CE Primary School, Grantham

What Am I?

My first letter is in house and also in thrilled.
My second sounds like a baby cheering.
My third is in Peter and also in pipe.
My fourth is in pee but not in he.
My fifth is in you but not in loo.

What am I?
A: Happy.

Jessica Marie Atkinson
St Sebastian's CE Primary School, Grantham

What Emotion Am I?

My first letter is in hat but not in mat
My second letter is in ant and in pants
My third letter is in pet but not in tent
My fourth letter is in pee but not in bee
My fifth letter is in yes and in yet.

What emotion am I?
A: Happy.

Tegan Olivia Cameron (9)
St Sebastian's CE Primary School, Grantham

A Riddle

I am mighty and strong,
I am sometimes a bit scared,
I am courageous and powerful,
I am as strong as a mountain lion.

What am I?
A: Brave.

Freddie Fowler (8)
St Sebastian's CE Primary School, Grantham

POETRY EMOTIONS - Eastern England

What Emotion Am I?

I scream with happiness,
I smile like your mouth,
Jumping with yellow,
I make everyone smile.

What emotion am I?
A: Joyful.

Corey Bennett
St Sebastian's CE Primary School, Grantham

What Emotion Am I?

I feel down-hearted,
My favourite thing is broken hearts
And I have a gloomy shadow.
I am crest-fallen.

What emotion am I?

Javan Mawu Elom Agboh (7)
St Sebastian's CE Primary School, Grantham

Sad

When I'm sad
It's like a rain cloud.

People call me names
It feels like I want to go
To the land of Forgetfulness.

No one loves me
I wonder what's going to happen next
But I'm not excited yet.

Mai Li
The Phoenix School, Willburton

Scared

Scary, spooky stories spook you out.
When it is dark it makes you sad.
Spiders creep up walls, they scare you with a shock.
Ghosts, white as wallpaper, they creep up on you
And scare you with a shout!

Deacon Jack Pattison (8)
The Phoenix School, Willburton

POETRY EMOTIONS - Eastern England

Happy

When I am happy I dance,
When I am happy I sing,
When I am happy I play a game,
When I am happy I paint.
These make me happy
So try these things
And they might make you happy too!

Ellen Stewart (8)
The Phoenix School, Willburton

Young Writers Information

We hope you have enjoyed reading this book – and that you will continue to in the coming years.

If you're a young writer who enjoys reading and creative writing, or the parent of an enthusiastic poet or story writer, do visit our website www.youngwriters.co.uk. Here you will find free competitions, workshops and games, as well as recommended reads, a poetry glossary and our blog.

If you would like to order further copies of this book, or any of our other titles, then please give us a call or visit **www.youngwriters.co.uk.**

Young Writers
Remus House
Coltsfoot Drive
Peterborough
PE2 9BF
(01733) 890066 / 898110
info@youngwriters.co.uk

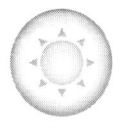